I Came

Part One of

A Trilogy

Part One – I Came
Part Two – That Ye Might Have
Part Three – Life More Abundant

Other Writings by Walter Lanyon

2 A. M. ◆ Abd Allah, Teacher, Healer

And It Was Told of a Certain Potter

Behold the Man ◆ Demonstration

Embers ◆ The Eyes of the Blind

The Impatient Dawn

Impressions of a Nomad

It Is Wonderful ◆ The Joy Bringer

A Lamp unto My Feet

The Laughter of God ◆ Leaves of the Tree

A Light Set upon a Hill

Life More Abundant

London Notes and Lectures

Out of the Clouds

Quintology: Ask and Ye Shall Receive

A Royal Diadem

The Temple Not Made with Hands

That Ye Might Have ◆ Thrust in the Sickle

Treatment ◆ Without the Smell of Fire

Your Heritage

Available through:
Mystics of the World
Eliot, Maine
www.mysticsoftheworld.com

I Came

Part One of
A Trilogy

Walter C. Lanyon

Part One – I Came
Part Two – That Ye Might Have
Part Three – Life More Abundant

I Came

Mystics of the World First Edition 2014
Published by Mystics of the World
ISBN-13: 978-0692337271
ISBN-10: 069233727X

For information contact:
Mystics of the World
Eliot, Maine
www.mysticsoftheworld.com

Cover graphics by Margra Muirhead
Printed by CreateSpace
Available from Mystics of the World and Amazon.com

Walter C. Lanyon, 1887 – 1967
Originally published 1940

The message
in this book
is lovingly dedicated
to Grace W.
and her daughter
Grace W.

"My son, some kings are commonplace, and not all laborers are worthy of their hire. But this I say to you: that if you are in league with gods, to learn life and to live it, neither kings nor commoners can prevent you, though they try their utmost. You shall find help unexpectedly, from strangers who, it may be, know not why."

—"Tsiang Samdup" in *The Devil's Guard*

Contents

Be still.
Be very still and deeply quiet.
You are a Living Soul.
It is well with thee.

—Walter C. Lanyon

Chapter I

The Mask of Personality

In ancient times, when the Greek nobleman wished to enact a role upon the stage, he donned a plaster mask representing either tragedy or comedy, thus saving himself the trouble and displeasure of distorting his features and instantly conveying to his audience the character he represented. If he wore a tragic mask, he passed through the play on that note and was recognized as a tragedian. Yet all the while, he might be smiling behind the mask.

When *you* left the Garden of Eden, you took on a mask, or persona (from which comes our word *personality*), and since that time you have changed from one mask to another throughout the ages. You chose the particular mask or character that you are now playing because you saw in it a possibility of accomplishing that which your Soul desired to express, irrespective of what that mask contained within itself. A thousand actresses have played Lady Macbeth, but each has brought out a different character.

The Immortal You, or Permanent Identity, took on mortality in order to bring to the surface a clear manifestation of Soul. But so often, in entering into the character of the mask, the You is hypnotized by the appearances of that character to such an extent that it finally is ruled by the mask. Thus, we see it very much in the same light as if the Greek nobleman, who was actually free from most cares of life, suddenly took on the tragic aspect of the mask he wore, thereby putting himself through all sorts of evil situations; or, if he wore the comic mask, becoming the fool or nitwit represented by that mask.

Jesus, the carpenter, discovered the limitations and inability to cope with life or personality (in His case called "Jesus"). "I can of myself do nothing." Discovering His true identity, He appropriated His heritage (made in the image and likeness of God), thereby freeing Himself from the limitations of (the mask) Jesus. He became so conscious of His Permanent Identity, with its fourth-dimensional power, God, that He was willing to go through all problems and beliefs of the "mask" of Jesus before He finally stepped it up to the place of Oneness — the "Touch me not" place above all human law or contact. By this recognition, He was able to cause the mask (Jesus) to do things that it could not possibly do. His field of expression and activity was always in the direction of the impossible.

So conscious of this "mind which was also in Christ Jesus" was He that He even allowed the "mask" to be crushed, broken, crucified, and put to death, in order that He might prove the power which lay within the Permanent Identity and which is indigenous to every man when he is able to recognize it. As soon as you discover this, you will understand the power to "pick it up or lay it down." Only by discovering or recognizing the Permanent Identity of *you* — the changeless creation of God — will you be able to assume command over the personality-mask.

Once you grasp this fundamental truth, you will really go within and shut the door, ceasing to judge further from appearances because you will have recognized the truth regarding them, as revealed by Jesus Christ, "Judge not from appearances."

Anything you then discover in your Permanent Identity becomes a reality in the relative world. In other words, whatever you discover as being true in this God-Consciousness makes itself manifest in and through you. Jesus became conscious of substance unlimited and was able to bring through the increase of bread and fish after having clearly stated, "I (Jesus) can of mine own self do nothing."

The mask, personality, "John Smith," can do nothing outside its own limitations. It has a very limited destiny and must and will follow it through. There is no escape unless the recognition of the Permanent Identity — the Christ within, or the Father-Consciousness — is made. At no time can the Jesus-mask cause the Father to do His bidding or to work "wonders" for the gratification of human curiosity. In every instance, He must "go unto the

Father"—ascend to His God-Consciousness, or Permanent Identity.

The mask, or personality, has already done everything it could to make it a success. Only after the recognition of the Permanent Identity (you), are you able to cause so-called miracles or the impossible to take place.

All this is above the reasoning or thought-taking process of the personality. "The wisdom of man is foolishness." The mask of tragedy can play only tragedy. The mask of sickness can produce only sickness. So with poverty, maladjustments, etc., there is very little that can actually be done about it. You may in some manner change the outside appearance a little, but if you wear the tragic mask, tragedy will mark the entire expression of your personality.

This thinking, or rather, "mis-thinking" mind, is designated as "a liar and the father of it." Its intelligence is exactly the same grade as that of a person who would consider any character or situation on the stage as real and unchangeable. The moment the play is over, the whole picture breaks up; the actors throw off their masks and become themselves.

The moment you understand the law of Jesus Christ, you discover the same ability within yourself and begin to throw off the mask of personality, and you are not so easily taken in, as it were, by what the character in the play is apparently doing. You begin to see, even if vaguely, that you have power "to pick it up or lay it down" by reason of the Permanent Identity, which changes not and which is "a temple not made with hands, eternal in the heavens."

There is nothing very strange about this. The fact of the matter is, it is so simple it is "given unto the child" and withheld from the adult (adulterous man), who is hypnotized to the extent that he builds everything on what the tragic mask represents— hence his sin, sickness, and death. It is glorious and wonderful when you first glimpse this revelation, for suddenly you feel a real awakening, a real movement towards your Permanent Identity. In this consciousness you discover, or rediscover, that which was always yours.

This discovery brings forth many things you have forgotten that were "shown to you on the Mount" and will change manifestations with lightning rapidity and ease—"in the twinkling of an eye, all shall be changed." The moment you see it in this Permanent Identity, it becomes visible in the manifest world.

Literally, then comes the revelation, "Whatsoever you tell the Father in secret shall be called from the housetops." Whatsoever you can accept in the Permanent Identity as real and true will be made visible in the manifest world. The Greek nobleman knows the difference between himself and the mask and is free. So with you. You are beginning to see the difference between your personality and your individuality. You are being "born again." It is wonderful!

Who are you then? Answer me. Are you tragedy? Are you comedy? Are you sickness, poverty, ingratitude? Or are you the *Christ of God?*

"Who do you say that I am? Answer me."

"Judging by the mask, some say you are John Smith or Mable Jones, that you are a thief, a liar, a crook, a holier-than-thou."

But, "Who do *you* say that I am?"

Do you begin to see why it is necessary actually to go within and shut your door?

This time you are returning or entering into the Father-Consciousness, and you need not be surprised at the many wonderful things taking place. Things will now happen with ease and dispatch, and you will find yourself moving in new levels of manifestation.

Small wonder, then—"Judge not from appearances, but judge righteous judgment." Judging from appearances leads only to a conclusion of evil, for the mask is tragic, the role is cast, and nothing can be done about it. The sooner you realize this the quicker you will stop trying to do anything with the mask outside and will enter into the Courts of the Lord and be your Permanent Self; and from that point on, you will see the useless and inane measurement of things by human thought. Human thought is a capacity of the personality, or mask, and is concerned almost wholly with evil, filled with anxiety and fear, which are without power to stop evil.

"When I would do good, I do evil." This is a sample of human thought-taking. No matter what be the power behind the mask, so long as you are hypnotized by it, you cannot manifest anything but the limitations of that mask. A lion has been raised to be afraid of a poodle dog. Maybe you are afraid of something equally simple.

Ceasing to judge from appearances, then, is not merely hiding from your eyes so-called pictures of evil, as if the so-called lion were to hide from the picture of the poodle, but it is a sudden ability to "judge righteous judgment" — that is, to see the pictures of sin, disease, etc., for what they are instead of what they appear to be; to look through the mask of personality and discover what is within.

The nobleman may be smiling radiantly behind this mask. Your Permanent Identity may be doing the same thing. So "look again" and see through the mask and enter into your true fulfillment. It is the recognition of this that saves you from the sudden thrusts of other personalities, or masks, in the Play of Life and protects you from the ugly and apparently inevitably disastrous results of human destiny.

So hypnotized have you been by this mask-personality which you are wearing that you even consult it regarding all the issues of life, and this mask then assumes such complete authority that it holds you, against all desire and better judgment, into a place of evil. No wonder Jesus said, "Awake thou that sleepest, and Christ (Permanent Identity) shall give thee light." Awake and arise from the dead! (mask of personality, John Smith) and go into the New Day with confidence!

You will understand how it is that the king can play the beggar but the beggar cannot play the king. The beggar may take on a veneer of spirituality or kingliness, show a few tricks of this pseudo-power, but his terrific handicaps are seen and discovered, and he is cast out as false. The mask of personality can never become the nobleman. He may take on a certain semblance of power and authority, but it is only an appearance which he cannot long sustain.

You cannot change the mask from without; you cannot heal it. Its innate capacities will stay with it so long as it must depict a role separate from the nobleman's identity. Every time the nobleman puts it on, he is temporarily, at least to the world of appearances, that thing. Every time Jesus allowed himself to operate under the Jesus-mask, He was a carpenter. The moment He made his assumption, He became Jesus Christ and did what the world called miracles, or things He could not otherwise have done.

Unlike the mask, the personality is, in its essential nature, plastic and fluidic, and that is the reason why Jesus, in entering into his Permanent Identity, could change the mask and cause it to sidestep its own destiny or limitations. So the hard-set mask of *you*, which appears so destined to perform evil, can be changed and its hateful destiny obliterated. To the human thought, this is impossible, and it cannot be done by thought. "Take no thought."

Do you begin to see why Mary "magnified the Lord within her" instead of trying to change anything about the Mary-mask? Do you begin to see why you will suddenly stop trying to change things on the outside? Then you will find the real place of revelation and thereby control the situation, causing the mask to change its appearance likewise. All this is filled with Light.

I am writing to you at dawn, and at this very moment, a terrific noise assaults my ears. Looking out, I perceive that the great walls of the old Hippodrome Theatre, a former landmark of New York City, have crashed to the ground. Workmen are razing the building that seemed so massive and enduring. Now, even as I watch, it is no more. Five minutes ago it was there. Now, as I return to my writing, it is done away with—gone forever. So one day will the walls of your personality, in their hard-set form, give way to the Christ-Consciousness so completely that the belief in sickness, age, poverty, and hurt shall be wiped out forever.

"You shall run and not be weary." Why? How? Do you know any athlete who can do it? Just what is it we are talking about, anyway? Was Jesus a sooth-sayer or a liar? You answer it. When you discover your Permanent Identity, if it be necessary, you shall run and not be weary, for you will know that the mask-personality has no longer intelligence or power of its own, no capacity to become tired, worn-out, sick, poor, unhappy, aged, or any of the so-called evils. None of this can be proven for the idle curiosity of disbelievers or people who want a sign. It is not for this purpose. It is a natural law that functions along natural lines when it becomes *natural* to you and ceases to be some fantastic, intangible, invisible power.

The use of the mask by the nobleman does not diffuse the mask in any way, and so you begin to sense-feel your fatigueless body. It cannot be overworked, for this newly recognized power can work faster through it than the body can possibly work by itself, with its muscular and mental limitations. The Power can speed up the use of muscles and nerves to such a capacity as is entirely impossible humanly.

We are moving to the realm of the capital wisdom of God, which is our heritage; otherwise, the teachings of Jesus are vain. Are you beginning to appropriate this power and experience the direct and instant action of it?

"Be still, and know that I am God." You can know this only in the place of your Permanent Identity, hence, if *I* am to speak, the Jesus-mask is used to see through, and actually his mouth becomes the mouth of God for the moment. If you can once see this, you will never again begin any task or work without a moment's pause for the recognition that it is "already done." With this recognition, a super-capacity comes to you which makes it possible to accomplish the hitherto impossible.

Chapter II

Behold, I Come Quickly

Behold, I come quickly,
and my reward is with me.

The reward, like the answer to prayer, is "before you ask." This is so entirely beyond the ken of humanity that nothing but confusion results from an attempt to *think* it out. There is nothing in all your human thinking or intellect that can conceive of an answer before the request or question is asked, and so, when the confusion has subsided, the whole thing is charged off to illusion or, if some manifestation has taken place, to "supernatural."

Supernatural is exactly what it is. It is not only above the human man but above his ability to understand. He cannot *stand* to have the very foundations of his human kingdom, governed under his so-called laws, rocked to the very foundation by the "coming quickly" into manifestation of this new dimension of power. Even to hear of it incites his anger—hence, the crucifixion.

Think of it—a child can do it and you cannot. Maddening, isn't it? It throws you into a fury of helpless anger. You want to fight or destroy such a person and his works. "Let us crucify him!" Yes, crucify the one saying there is abundance in our apparent poverty, there is health in our sickness, there is happiness in our inharmony. Get rid of such a doctrine! "Why have you come here to disturb us?"

"I bring not peace, but a sword," and this sword is sharply felt when human thinking, with its vicious circle of ideas, comes into contact with it. It pierces the very heart of every cherished belief. Man has striven for years to establish his idea of heaven on earth, and he sees the order of his life crumbling.

Because you and ten thousand like you and also ten thousand great leaders and teachers and wise-heads have found sickness, sin, and death to be true, this does not change the fact that "one with God is a majority." "Ten thousand may fall at thy right hand, but it shall not come nigh thee because ... " Because what? Because you have entered into your oneness with God.

Trying to demonstrate over the appearance of ten thousand beliefs in evil is a hopeless job — *trying* to do anything spiritual is hopeless. You cannot control or use the God-power as you would a fire hose on a burning building. The sooner you find out that you cannot control God by your thinking, by your affirmation, by your courses of lessons the sooner you will begin to "let." This letting is not a supine waiting for something to happen. It is a conscious merging with your Permanent Identity. "I and my Father are one."

Either the wisdom of man is foolishness in the eyes of God or else it is wisdom. If you find it to be wisdom, then you must place your entire faith in it. If it is true, there is no reason to change it. Hence, to try to get rid of evil, which is a part of the human thinking, is foolishness. If evil were a part of God and He destroyed it, He would be literally destroying Himself.

You see that we have come to a place beyond all metaphysical theories, past all New Thought systems, and into pure Consciousness; past all the ancient wisdom of the old worlds and their myriad ways of getting into heaven. Through the revelation of Jesus Christ, we enter into a permanent state of things—the "before Adam was, I am," right back to "in the beginning" of *you*.

Not nearly so difficult as it appears. All these thousands of years are but a day in the mind of God, so you have been in this ugly miasma of evil only a few days, though a single day of one of these many centuries may seem as a thousand years to you. All the illusions which so long have bound you will melt into oblivion at His coming, for "the former things have passed away; behold, all things are made new." The former things shall not be remembered or come into mind anymore. It is marvelous, this awakening to the new order that now is establishing itself in you.

It is direct action because it is operating from the ceaseless fount of power. You speak not of yourself but directly from Him who sent you into expression. So your voice becomes the God-voice, and you speak the unique word that will bring release to the captive. You can never think what this word should be; that is entirely in the hands of your Permanent Identity. "Open your mouth, and I will supply the word." You are emerging gently or suddenly (depending on the degree of your appropriation of the Father-Consciousness) into the very Presence to such a degree that you take the literal word *Jesus Christ* as your Word.

If you do not talk *of* and *about* the truth, you will have no challengers asking you to change stones into bread or some other ridiculous thing. There is a great difference in talking *of* and *about* the truth and *speaking* the truth. When you talk of and about the truth, you are always speaking in the past or future tense. When you *speak the truth,* you are in the present tense. In other words, you are speaking the Word. If you persist in talking of and about the truth, even when called upon to make the most trifling "demonstration" you will not be able to do so. Remember, the power is not "proven" to satisfy the curiosity of unbelievers. It is made manifest automatically whenever you "touch" Me, to "make your joy full."

The power is exact and as natural in its functions as mathematics. The law of mathematics is not affected by climate, nationality, beliefs, opinions, wars or rumors of wars, complete chaos, or ten million other beliefs of man. Neither is the law of God affected and, when understood, is found to be as intact and as operative as mathematics. There is nothing emotional, sentimental, or in any way biasing in this law of God, which Jesus so perfectly explained as the law of Life. This wonderful law may run through and touch at points many orthodox religious beliefs, but it has nothing to do with them. They have to do with it. God is non-sectarian, impersonal, not depending in any way on any organization. All organizations are merely shadows of the personalities which originated them.

It took an earthquake to get Peter out of prison. Perhaps it may take this for you, but at no time does it make any difference how mortal man, mortal thinking, mortal belief are upset. If you stand in your new consciousness, the "jailers" must run for their lives; but afterwards they must come and literally invite you to come out of the prison of human belief into which they have cast you. It is amazing how they must "eat their own words."

So is it with every hellish and fiendish device or person that is fashioned against you. It is wonderful! "Stand fast and see the salvation of the Lord." Nothing is difficult to this Power.

"The word of God is quick, and powerful, and sharper than a two-edged sword," turning in all directions. Do you hear? *The word of God.* Not the words of man, which are ten thousand affirmations and beliefs, but the word of God is quick and powerful and sharper, sharper than a two-edged sword turning in all directions. Ponder this—a two-edged sword swirling about you in all directions. And so, You are the Word of God made manifest, and the consciousness of this will decapitate any human thought formation. Nothing can stand in the way of this Word (sword), for these things are true.

Yet if you are thinking to fight evil, sickness, lack with your sword, you are thwarted. You are told, "You do not need to fight." "Put up your sword." "He that takes the sword shall perish by the sword."

All of this seems paradoxical, but there is not a contradiction in the whole statement. There is no war in God. War is in the mind of man. The coming of God into manifestation displaces the evil appearances of man-thinking. Hence, "I bring not peace, but a sword," and at the same time, "I come not to destroy, but to fulfill." These statements are one and the same thing. Nothing is destroyed but the congested thinking of the human mind. The wicked human thought has congealed into icebergs of sickness, sin, poverty, inharmony, which are melted out of existence and which are literally destroyed by the presence or recognition of this God-power.

One thing is sure: the moment you step up, you *are* this Presence. Evil must either disintegrate or disappear from your present life, whether it (the evil) represents person, place, or thing. Nothing shall stand in the way of this on-coming through you. It (the evil) can then no longer live in your world.

Throwing out ballast causes a balloon to enter a new level of atmosphere. As the balloon ascends, outlines of people and places seem less important and less distinct, and finally only geometric patterns remain. So with you. As you ascend (which is not a *physical* upward movement but a blending or liaison with the Presence) the forms and outlines of evil fade out of existence and eventually lose all their force or power as such.

The moment you, in your new God-given Identity, come into the presence of sin, sickness, or death, it must and will disappear from your present life. It may no longer live in your world. Anything that touches you will cause the "virtue" to come out of you and bring the unmanifest into being. This is automatic. You are actually beginning to appropriate that which belongs to you. As formerly you desired to heal, now you cannot refrain healing anything that touches you.

What you have in your consciousness, you have in your manifest world—and only that. You cannot possibly get rid of a thing, person, place, or condition in your manifest world if it is not first released in your consciousness. When you "loose a thing in heaven" (consciousness), it is *bound* to manifest itself on the earth. You have freed it into expression—this God-power—and it is, so to speak, bound into manifestation. As you free or move freely in the substance of God, it is bound or shaped into the form of supply needed in your everyday life, whatever that may be—money, clothes, food, friends, etc.

To the human mind, this may seem difficult, for there are many things in your manifest world of which you say you have never even thought. If you had not recognized them in your consciousness, there could be no possible way for them to exist in manifestation. Whether we like this or not, it is so. "All that the Father (your consciousness of God in yourself) has is mine." Every manifestation in your world—good, bad, or indifferent—is held in place by your consciousness of it. Destroying manifestation does not destroy the idea; as long as it remains in consciousness, it will find an embodiment. A man who commits murder finds he is not rid of his victim but lives with him as never before.

Awake; arise; go within and ponder these things. Hiding or shutting a thing away does not get rid of it. You must strip it of its supposed power by taking away its only substance—your belief in it. The moment you cut off your thinking from an evil situation, it will disintegrate and disappear, so we do not handle disease or financial loss or lack or woes as we were formerly taught to do.

We are awakening to the consciousness of the Presence, through the revelation of Jesus Christ, and this awakening brings us out of much mental hypnotism. The time was, when we believed that to mention a disease by its Adam name was to give it power. We called it a "belief" or a "claim" and imagined that by not calling it a name we made it less real. "Awake thou that sleepest, and Christ shall give thee light."

There is a wonderful spiritual exaltation which will come to you when you know you have *instant* contact with the Father within. You can call upon Him *now*, no matter what your former idea was regarding "systems" of getting in touch with Him.

Now! You are *instantly* in touch with Him and are *experiencing* the whole glorious flow of the Presence passing through your temple-body into expression. No matter what is confronting you, you can get your immediate answer and instant assurance of, "Behold, I come quickly, and my reward is with me," and in a moment experience relief from whatever may be the human-thought difficulty.

You are beginning to behold the glorious power that is yours through the recognition of Jesus Christ. No matter where this finds you or what the condition, you now can and will "speak the word." You can and will "smite the rock." You can and you will "cause the desert to blossom as a rose," and you can and you will now do all the other wonderful things of which Jesus spoke. It is good for you to remember that one man did it all, proved it all for you. "Let that mind be in you which was also in Christ Jesus."

It seems too good to be true, and that is why it *is* true—true to *you* if you can take it; true if you can accept it and turn once and for all from the human belief of good and evil. "Behold, I come quickly," so much more quickly than any human action, even more quickly than human thought. The speed of human thought is as slow as a paralyzed man compared with this quickness with which *I* come to dissolve the pictures of evil about you.

Chapter III

Breaking Patterns

Former things have passed away;
behold, all things are become new.

Former ideas about truth are yielding to the new order, the New Day. Old patterns are recognized as false and are crumbling away, disintegrating before the Presence, the Life, the new Revelation. It is wonderful! The moment you "see" with the spiritual eye, you will perceive there is no more healing to take place, only revelation. In the new state of awareness, every time you recognize your Father-Consciousness, you change the pattern of the Son. In other words, when you perceive the Permanent Consciousness of the changeless Father, then the changing, shifting nature of *John Smith* breaks the old pattern and shows forth a new design.

This merging with the Father caused the patterns of limitation about Jesus to disintegrate, to fall apart, as it were. When the new vision or idea or pattern was established, then the atoms or elements integrated again, as though they were particles of steel drawn into place by a magnet.

The moment you see what takes place in this new consciousness, at that moment you will stop *trying* to heal the body or to change the expression of it. Transfiguration does not deal with cured, helped, or healed bodies. It is a completely new pattern that suddenly integrates out of the elements and forms of the former pattern.

It is true that you cannot make a block of ice into a sphere without first crushing it, thereby losing its transparency. It is possible, after a fashion, to change its shape, but that is difficult. If, however, the ice is melted, the water can be poured into any mold desired and frozen again. This is a poor illustration, but it will suffice for the moment and will give some idea of what Jesus indicated was in the grasp of every man who recognized it.

It is written in the law: "Who by taking thought can add one cubit to his stature?" and the command, "Go into all the world; take no thought about the robe, body, purse."

Why this admonition? Because taking thought about all the ways and means and things in the universe has not helped you to get any of them. Those old hypnotic thought patterns are the models of ice that must be melted down instead of being changed, in order that the new design may appear.

Do you understand why the thought-taking process, in the ordinary sense of the word, cannot change the body or the effect of the word on the body? At best it can only bring on a form of self-hypnosis. Trying to cure the body by thought is like trying to change the form of a block of ice—you may accomplish a little something, but the results gained from working from the outside are practically nil.

But in your new awareness of the Light of the Son-Father and the Holy Ghost, you find out what is taking place when the Light comes through. You become a new creature of the Christ Jesus.

Do you understand what "a new creature" means? It is not the block of ice chiseled into a new shape, the old body patched up, the new wine in old bottles. It is a complete disintegration of the hard, fast thought-picture manifestations which you have had and the integration into the new idea—"the picture shown to you on the mount."

Every knee shall finally bend at the name (nature) of Jesus Christ. It is well with you. It is wonderful! For even as I write these words, this very agreement is taking place between us; you have only to recognize this in me, to reach out and touch Me and receive the blessing. Do you hear? The stir of the risen Lord within you will cause you to be filled with joy.

An eagle flying swiftly over the chasm on its great strong wings is a far cry from the unhatched egg lying in the nest on the mountain peak. Within that eagle egg is contained an urge to fly. It is possible for the egg to fly through the air, of course—not of its own volition, but nevertheless, it could, after a fashion, experience a sensation of flying by being thrown. It could never, however, take off by its own power, even though the urge within were very strong.

Thus with you. In the Sonship degree of consciousness, you are filled with longings for health, happiness, wealth, and expression; but though you have the urge to acquire these ideals, so well-developed that it seems only a question of willpower and grit to obtain them, yet with your present equipment it is as impossible for you to do it as it is for an egg to fly.

The pattern of consciousness must be changed in order that these things may take form in your life. They must have a new vehicle to bring them into expression, a new shape, as it were, of consciousness. With all its intense urge from within, the egg cannot fly, even though it were covered with feathers and made to appear as an eaglet. "Marvel not ... ye (yes, you) must be born again" in order that the new level of spirituality to which you are ascending may find a consciousness which can take high-powered instructions and bring you by "a way ye know not of."

It is marvelous! As this word is being written, the room is filled with Light, all of which will pour out on you; and you will find something new—a stirring within, an awakening, and a tendency to sing within—an inner awareness which is suddenly arousing itself. Just as in the legends, when the Prince touched the lips of the Sleeping Beauty, a great stirring, a great awakening was suddenly brought to the whole castle and estates—life and joy began to express themselves in the new day, the new pattern—so the Prince of Revelation has touched your lips, and you are awakening from the death-sleep induced by the hypnotism of human thinking. It is wonderful!

When the urge for life is felt in the egg, there is a stirring, a cry within, "Give me a body." Just so, when the urge for the beautiful and happy things in life is felt within you, a cry comes up from the depths, "Give me a body." You are starved to death because you have been feeding on the husks of symbolic phenomena. You are worn out with symbolic wealth, which you say you possess but can spend only in imagination. It, too, is constantly crying out, "Give me a body; give me a body." It is wonderful, this crying out of the unborn within you. The children cry out from the loins for expression, "Give me a body."

So the egg rests under the warmth of the mother bird, and from the instant the center of it is touched with the warmth of love, something has started. What has started? The pattern plan is beginning to form, and that very forming of the new consciousness is going to break the shell of the old design and change the egg into a bird. Still will it be an egg, for it has lost nothing but has absorbed the entire substance of the egg; yet in its new expression it is not egg. So is it with you when you are absorbed into the Christ-Consciousness. You are no more *you* as of old, yet are you—but no longer under the curse which formerly governed you.

The egg is under the curse of the law of chance. It is acted upon even as unenlightened man is acted upon by human destiny. Neither he nor the egg has capacity to get out of the way of danger. He may try it, but more than likely he will move into the path of destruction. An egg cannot move out of the way of oncoming destruction; yet, as the bird, it has full capacity to do so. Thus, the new pattern you are to bring out is the thing that will save you from being acted upon by all the false beliefs you have about you.

The old pattern of a diseased or worn-out body is acted upon by the beliefs of disease or age, and nothing can be done about it. These outside forces which have been established by being accepted are there for one purpose, and that is your destruction. Nothing in the human thought can stop this, except temporarily, for this is human destiny that must be fulfilled in that degree of consciousness.

Do you begin to see why Jesus came saying, "You must be born again," and why He made constant reference to the new-borning process of life, referring always to changing of the pattern instead of patching up the old design; to disintegration of human thought-pictures and reintegration of spiritual manifestation?

When heat permeates a grain of popcorn, it is so filled with warmth that it automatically bursts into a new pattern. It cannot help itself once it is subjected to sufficient heat. So is it with you. Once you subject yourself to God, you cannot help or stay the change, the transformation, that is bound to take place. It is automatic and is something that cannot be stayed. It is the evolving thing, the wonderful quickening of the power which destroys all former limitation. "Behold, I make all things new," even your body and your world.

You now see that we possess nothing that makes for bondage but do possess all things for use and joy. The law of integrity which says, "Be careful about nothing," and at the same time says, "Pick up the pieces; see that nothing be lost," is the glorious freedom of Spirit. This Spirit is not wasteful, profligate, destructive, but lavish to such an extent that It will flow over all the earth—the great gush of life.

In the jungle, where growth is so prolific that one can almost hear it, every available inch of ground and space is filled with expression—trees and vines and flowers, luscious fruits, gorgeous birds—yes, the whole of creation is heaped up, is pressed down, is crowded together, is running over with manifestations. So is it with your "desert" body, which suddenly becomes a point of expression where all manifestation must and will come through into being. "Yet in my flesh shall I see God."

Your body (temple) is the point of contact between the seen and the unseen, and it is only through your body that the power can be stepped down into visibility, bringing your finest fulfillment into manifestation, actually giving you your heart's desire. It is only when the sacredness of this wonderful life comes to you that this can be achieved. It is not possible so long as you are playing around with the human idea, trying to impress someone or to show what you can do. It is true you might *have* to be famous. It is nothing to be sought for, but you might be called into that expression. If so, you can handle it if you are willing to let your consciousness be stayed on the Power and take no personal credit or blame.

It is wonderful what this new revelation is bringing through to us *at this moment*. You are beginning to see why you should "come out from among them and be separate." This is not a hiding away of the body but a hiding away of the "pearl of great price." You will not lack recognition when the time comes, and it will be recognition of the right sort because a luminous, soft, white light of that pearl of great price will shine forth and be brighter than the noonday of all human power or glory. Do you see why there must be secrecy?

Do you begin to see how, in the hypnosis of the human mind, the temple (John Smith) has grown into a place of power (imaginary, of course), stupidly assuming the ability to do, to create, and to change things? Then suddenly the John Smith finds that he has no real power, and that even more, the John Smith temple can be used for anything. It can be the stomping ground for all sorts of evil and sickness; it can be filled with all sorts of disease; it can be filled with filthy parasitic growth— and he can do nothing about it. His body is susceptible to all this so long as it is run on the *thought* plan. Comes the revelation of the Trinity, and then the pattern is completely changed in order that the new consciousness may be a fit dwelling place for the Lord.

Do you begin to see now what it means to "be still, and know that I am God," instead of trying to change things, to change the shape of the ice or to patch up the old garments? When you appropriate this revelation, your body is automatically trans-figured by the presence of this Fatherhood degree. It is changed and made flesh and made new. "And the glory of the Lord fills the house" (consciousness), and it comes out through all the openings of the temple. Every atom of expression is filled with Light, and you find your temple (John Smith) illumined. The struggle is over.

"Who told you you were naked (stripped of all the necessary things for your happiness)?" Why, *he, she, it, but, if,* and *maybe.* They all told you, and they will keep on telling you until this whole plan of human thought is finally disintegrated by the blending with the Father.

All the lovely talents you possess—"for every man has his gift"—all the glorious *you* that has failed to come forth is saved in this disintegrating process. The elements which have solidified about you as a pattern of evil are now disassociated and are reshaped into a new and perfect design. The grain of wheat smothered in a bushel of chaff has suddenly come into its own; it has fallen into the ground and rotted so that it could be made alive, so that it could change the pattern into a form which could carry out its new desires.

So is your awakening to take place. How do I know? Because this message that I am writing was written for you—*you*, the reader—at this very moment. If it were not so, you would not now be pausing in holy contemplation; you would not be praising God that He had so spoken to you out of the pages of a book.

Do you hear—you who read? Do you begin to see how the smashing of these obsolete patterns is taking place?

In a strange and fantastic way, the old theology of orthodoxy really believed in smashing patterns, but they thought it could be accomplished only through physical death. They knew that in order to enter heaven man had to change his present pattern and that the only way to do it was to throw off the body. But in the light of the present revelation, we adhere to the word of Jesus Christ when He says, "Here and now."

And how does this necessary disintegration take place? The Lord says, "Not by thought, not by might, not by power, but by my spirit." By the spirit of this recognized Father-Consciousness within you does this disintegration take place. As it begins to fall apart, you will find the light of this new revelation shining in its place, and the seal will be placed upon your lips. Your glorious talents and gifts will be freed from their imprisonment.

You can go into all the world. You can go into any land, and the moment you set up the temple within yourself, you are established. Do you hear? For you have all that it takes to establish this temple of expression. You can be in the desert or in the city, physically alone or with crowds. The moment you pitch your tent or set up your temple, your influence is felt. That is why you can cleanse the leper, raise the dead, heal the sick.

Do you begin to grasp the magnitude of this revelation? Transfigured, transformed by the uplifting of your consciousness—do you see? Do you hear?

> The New Day confronts you. You go your way secretly, powerfully, without the bondage of person, book, organization, or thing. You are free.

Chapter IV

First Person, Present Tense

Talking *of* and *about* truth, and *speaking the truth* are radically different things. The first is merely rehearsing the letter, which is dead and not effective. The latter is the "spake and it was done" state of consciousness. Jesus spoke the truth in the present tense and first person, and results, or manifestation, immediately followed. "He made himself as God." In other words, He spoke as one having authority because He spoke from the place of authority.

In spite of the fact that you profess to be a follower of Jesus Christ, you are afraid to make any direct statement of good without first knocking on wood. Why is this? On the other hand, it is quite common for people who even profess a knowledge of truth to exclaim over evil, "Just my luck ... it always happens to me ... I never knew it to fail," etc., etc. In other words, you are unable to say anything good that is positive.

For instance, you dare not say, "I shall be perfectly well this time next year ... I shall be abundantly supplied this time next year," because you are speaking always from the consciousness of John Smith, which knows, "When I would do good,

I do evil." "As for man, his days are few and full of trouble."

This is all due to the fact that you are talking of and about truth instead of speaking the truth. When you speak the truth because of your liaison with the Christ within, you can say definitely, "I will come and heal him," without any reservations, without any treatments, without any series of mental mechanics, because you speak with authority. There is no doubt about the results—you speak the word and it is done, as far as you are concerned. If the other person cannot accept the truth, that is his loss.

In order to practice the revelation as given to us by Jesus Christ, you must act from the standpoint of absolute authority. Very often you hear people "trying" to make a healing, using such terms as *we*, meaning, of course, "God and I," or "I and God," according to the importance of the individual. The most one in this state of mind can get out of talking of and about the truth is personal adulation or an emotional thrill which soon disappears.

Taking Jesus as an example, we see in every instance of healing that He made an assumption of his Fatherhood degree of understanding. Hence, He could make a clear statement of facts without equivocation, without fear of contradiction—a straightforward speaking of the Word: "I will come and heal him." It would be sheer folly or conceit in Jesus (or any other man) to say He could heal anything. Jesus knew this when He said, "I can of myself do nothing," *but*—and then the thrilling thing happens, when He merges this helplessness of human thought with the Divine and can explain, "but with God all things are possible."

It fairly makes you thrill with joy just to sense such a thing, even to read the *word*. If you *see*, you are suddenly filled with inspiration. Think of it— *but!* Jesus saying He could do nothing—helpless, hopeless—and then suddenly, "but with God all things are possible." Are you beginning to hear, to sense, to sense "all things"—not *some things*, not *a few things*, but *all things*? Do you hear? All things. Is that enough?

Now do you begin to see the necessity of being still and knowing that "I am God" rather than trying to make God demonstrate a new car or a red hat? If you are consciously with the Presence, then *all* things are possible, and the Voice which speaks through you is One in authority, and He is always speaking in the present tense and the first person. "For I also am a man under authority." This wonderful self-recognition of the centurion is exactly what is necessary for you to accomplish the works set for you to do and to hear the wonderful recognition, "I have not seen so great a thing; no, not in all Israel."

What authority could possibly be in a mind which was filled with quandary as to whether the

Power would heal or would not. "I will come and heal him" leaves no—not any—doubt.

Do you begin to see? Who are you, anyway?

"*This* is life eternal, to know Me." Do you want to know Me and experience life eternal? When you know *life*, you suddenly forget the ideas of "health and sickness" and "strength and weakness." These, together with all the other pairs of opposites, are merely parentheses on the circle of life, a segment of the whole. These pairs of opposites are merely the limitations placed on life by personality. They differ in every instance. What is strength to one man is positively weakness to another; what is abundance to one man is limitation to another. Yet God is All—whole—*One*.

A personality such as your John Smith has a limitation as to the placement of these parentheses, beyond which he cannot go. Jesus also had His great limitations and to such an extent that He explained, "I can of mine own self do nothing." As long as you are working with a consciousness which believes in health and sickness, your range of activity and expression is only between the parentheses, or your concept of life, which you place on the whole. You begin to see, therefore, why it is necessary to "go unto the Father."

"When you lose your life, you shall find it." When you lose your parentheses, you will find the universal Life, and inversely speaking, when you hold on to your life (parentheses), you will lose it. It can run only the length of your human belief.

The same thing is true regarding substance. Until you lose your personal limitation, you can have only that limited substance included in your parenthesis. A chicken that is not released from its shell dies the moment it has come to the limitation of the shell. So do you die when you come to the limits of your parentheses. Do you begin to understand why the apparently inane command is given to you, "Enlarge the borders of your tent ... ." "Launch out into deeper waters ... "—in other words, break through these parentheses of human limitations which you have imposed upon your life. "Come out from among them, and be ye free."

There must be a casting away of all bondage of former thought and a stepping into the revelation where the pairs of opposites exist no more. "When you lose your life, you shall find it." As a bucketful of dirty water thrown into the sea is instantly made clean, so your dirty life, filled with the history of every filthy thing, is suddenly made clean by breaking down the parentheses of limitation you have held about you. Jesus did this immediately when He "went unto His Father."

Life is *now*. In reality, it exists only in the eternal Present, and so if your manifestations are to be alive, they must be animated and sustained by life *now*. The mental plane talks about tomorrow and yesterday, things that have happened or things that might happen, but it never actually speaks of things taking place. All future, of course, is fraught with fear, fear of the deadly possibility of unpredictable evil. The slimy fear that crawls on its belly is always hiding in the grass, to strike suddenly in this thought-taking state. You are not giving up anything when you release your life into the God-Life.

"As for man, his days are few and full of trouble." If you believed this as true and didn't sense the possibility of something higher, why would you dare or wish to bring another being into existence? But then, in reality, you have never brought one into existence of your own volition or will, no matter how much praying or cursing you have done. You have neither created life nor kept it from manifestation. Eventually we begin to understand that life *expresses* whenever it has the least opportunity to do so and not at the bidding of man. There cannot be, therefore, such a thing as an illegitimate manifestation. It could be illegitimate only when it came under the hypocritical parenthesis of man's thought.

"He made himself as God" was one of the causes for which they crucified Jesus. Too late we found we had nailed nothing *real* to the "tree," for we discovered "He" was suddenly on the other side of the lake; that He had suddenly passed through the crowds. We discovered that He had power to call upon His Father and instantly be surrounded by twelve legions of angels. Why, that is one legion for every month in the year, and we are talking about angels, which are more powerful in their invisible state than a whole army of tanks and bomber planes—and *you* have the same power.

"Believest thou this?" Answer me. Yes, you. This funny little thing that has tried so hard to crucify life suddenly discovers it also has power at any time or place to call upon the Father and literally, factually, bring forth and surround itself with twelve legions of angels.

Do you hear? Do you believe?

"Awake thou that sleepest, and Christ shall give thee life." That Father within you—Permanent Identity—will give your poor little John Smith life and cause you to rise from a tomb of your own creation into the very presence of Life, filled with the very joys of heaven here and now.

No one may recognize you as a great soul—that is not important; but you may do most glorious things and have most thrilling manifestations. What do you care what the man "whose breath is in his nostrils" thinks, believes, or says about anything? "What is that to thee? Follow thou me." If he says the moon is made of green cheese or that sickness is real, that poverty is true, what is that to thee? Answer me.

When will you learn to put the coal of fire on your lips and "let the filthy be filthy still." If you believe in death, war, pestilence, and destruction as realities, you may get a chance to prove this though you are ten thousand miles from any battlefield. The fury of a war could happen in a small room, as far as you are concerned, as well as it could on a battlefront. Do you begin to see? Do you begin to hear? You may be one of the "ten thousand at your right hand," or you may be the *one*—that depends.

"Eyes have not seen (no eyes—not yours or the eyes of your teacher or your holy one), nor have their ears heard, nor has it yet entered into their hearts the things that are (right now) prepared." I said *prepared*, already prepared, right now.

So you begin to see that we are talking about a new state of consciousness. New capacities are released in you, new ways and means to bring out manifestations which are not listed and never have been listed in any book or course of instruction. Jesus merely glanced at the lepers and they were clean. Can you understand this? It can't be explained in three-dimensional words, and yet it is so.

When are you going to leave off all your filthy human thinking and follow Me? A glass of water can be transmuted into the elixir of life when offered to a sick man, that is, if it *can be,* and of course it cannot possibly be unless it can—and then it *can.* Do you understand what I am saying to you? It is all rather ridiculous, utter insanity in the eyes of man, since any chemist could grab the glass of water from your hand and find it was still water. The moment the human thought tries to put the God-power under the microscope of human belief, it finds nothing.

Again, this beautiful revelation of Jesus Christ is not brought into manifestation to satisfy the idle curiosity of disbelievers. It is a perfectly natural function of your Christ-Consciousness, and you have full and absolute right to it, but quite naturally you are beginning to see the need of secrecy and silence. Do not tell—*show*.

Aren't you thrilled with this revelation of your divinity? Do you begin to see how the speaking of the Word from this present tense, first-person state of consciousness brings about, or reveals, what before has been concealed?

What a lovely sense of authority and power! You pass along life's highway and answer the call of the divinity in another. Whoever touches you or calls upon you will receive automatically the agreement. Virtue will proceed out of you; the healing will take place. The beggar at the temple gates will arise, leap into the air and go on his way, shouting for joy. It is amazing!

Though ten lepers are healed, only one returns to give thanks or to make complete recognition and to establish the manifestation as a reality. The other nine have gone on their way. Undoubtedly they will, in their excitement, "salute" every man they pass on the highway, who will begin to tell them of the "facts" of leprosy as proven by ten million wiseheads; and at the end of the day, the nine will have ieprosy again and will charge it all off to a beautiful daydream. Do you begin to see the necessity of recognition?

"I was hungry, and you fed me. I was cold, and you clothed me." What for?

What else could I do, in the consciousness of *All?* When you enter a warm room, you take on automatically the temperature of that room. When you enter any degree of consciousness of God, you take on everything that is in that degree, and it is automatically embodied.

"God spake, and it was done." We are only beginning to understand that in the God-Consciousness, when a thing is done, *it is done.* Do you understand? There is no *maybe* or *perhaps*—it is *done.* Do you get the connection between this and the words of Jesus Christ, "It is done"?

"I say ... go, and he goeth; and ... come, and he cometh." Why? Is there any reason why a particle of steel in the proximity of a magnet instantly comes by the shortest possible way to the magnet? Do not imagine we can speak a word or a stream of words and accomplish anything. There is, "Peace, peace," and, "Lord, Lord," and yet nothing happens. Still, you are told to "only speak the word." *Only*—it seems as if someone were making light of the situation. You have tried so hard, yet it says to you, "Only speak the word." Do you hear?

Next time, why don't you speak the Word without knocking on wood? Are you afraid? Jesus made himself as God. Can you? He went through all the necessary steps to show the nothingness in all human belief and to relieve you from it all, but if you wish to go through the passions of Jesus and emotionally suffer all that He proved to be unnecessary, you may do so. You may even bring about a crucifixion. I shouldn't be surprised that you have said many times that you have been crucified. I know I have.

"Only speak the word, and my servant shall be made alive." All right then, "I will"—and the servant is healed the selfsame hour, at a distance physically, but in the Presence all the while. No time to give a treatment or argument or affirmation; no time to become spiritual or emotional or to reel off a lot of mantras, but speak the Word—not the words. Words are merely a human effort to express a state of consciousness which already is. Signs follow— they do not precede.

Do you understand? Or do you? Who are you, anyway, hiding behind a mask of personality? What do you want?

"As he is, so are we in this present world." *Present world*—mean anything to you? I said *present* world, not world to come. Do you believe it? "He made himself as God," a terrible thing to do. Better make yourself after some human god who is fast going into the dust. Copy some other human manifestation. Get one that is rich, famous, grand, a success man, a hero. Make yourself—but don't, for heaven's sake, make yourself as God.

Just as long as you will stay down on the human plane with misery and suffering, it is all right. "Let me go on with my silly beliefs in truth"—as the lady who *successfully* prayed for her little ailing chickens not to die was proud to say three months later, "Now they are big enough to eat." A lovely understanding of spiritual law has been invoked to avert the death of her chickens at one time in order that she might inflict it at her pleasure later on.

This story was told me in perfect sincerity as a proof of spiritual understanding. It made me ask myself, "What kind of praying are you doing, anyway?" And so I, in turn, ask you, "What kind of praying are you doing? Is it begging, beseeching? Is it an emotional outburst? Is it telling God how wonderful He is—something He probably already knows? Or is it in accordance with the law of Jesus Christ: "Be still, and know that *I* am nigh."

Signs follow. Do you hear? It says very definitely they follow—they do not precede. Surely, then, a sign must follow every prayer, and possibly so quickly that it is manifested before it is yet spoken. "Before they call, I will answer, and while they are yet speaking, I will give it unto them." This is what is known as *direct action;* it is in the present tense, and it is the *I*, the first person, who is doing it. When your Eye or "I" becomes *single,* then your whole embodiment and universe are filled with light.

This all seems to make one appear rather useless and dumb, as dumb as an ox for the slaughter. You begin to know nothing. You listen and listen until the time comes to speak and the Word is to be made manifest, and then—why, then all is changed in the twinkling of an eye. Yes, even the glance can do it, and the touch can do it, and the physical absence can do it because it is already done. It all happens automatically. No one is blamed or praised for the healing, and no system of metaphysics or teacher or organization is lauded to the sky.

"But this isn't fair; he was my patient ... I belong to a certain group ... they must have the credit ... I worked for him for thirty days." Imagine praying or speaking the Word and then telling the poor, benighted patient, "Come back tomorrow, and I will pray again." What a wretched state in which to send anyone away. What little faith in the power of your words. Imagine Jesus taking patients by the week or month. Funny, isn't it?

Present tense and first person: "Behold, I come quickly, and my reward is with me." It is not with somebody else, and it is not with tomorrow or the next day—it is with Me. You understand? My body accompanies Me. Can you take it? "Yes, I know, *but* ..."

When are you going to smash that prison door, that strange state of human thought that will go to the heights of revelation, in words at least, and in arguments for spirituality, then will suddenly do a nosedive into the valley of despair with these words: "Yes, I know, *but* ..." It would even go on recounting all sorts of things, acknowledging truth on the one hand but always finishing up with, "Yes, *but* ... "

The signs follow—naturally, normally—or else they upset your whole life with excitement. Many times people have told so often of the terrible things *they* overcame with *their* understanding that those things returned to them with accelerated force because whatever you magnify in your heart is going to come into manifestation, and if you magnify a past evil, it finally becomes stronger than your belief in God; hence, it apparently overcomes God, and you are back where you started.

Have you ever imagined Jesus giving a testimonial meeting, which for the most part is planned after the testimonial addenda in the back of a medicine almanac? "After taking three bottles ... After taking three treatments from Mrs. Blank ... ." Jesus had plenty to tell, but it was all so natural to Him that He never thought of explaining it into a "box-office" value.

"The works that I do, you shall do also, and even greater." Well! There you are. Why don't you try it? Because you have tried and have failed ignominiously. You even felt a little hurt about it because God didn't hear, and so you tried again and again and again, and then perhaps you said, "Well, it's too hard for me to understand." But a child can do it—because he *does* it instead of *trying* to do it, and therein lies the secret.

A recognition of this simple thing will bring about a housecleaning. All condemnation will be thrown out, all wondering about the past defeats and successes. The past is suddenly closed. You are entering into the dimension of "Thank you, Father," where the Cosmic Power urges a manifestation into being. It is this consciousness of the finished thing which causes you to say, "Thank you, Father," and is the power which steps down the unseen into visibility. As steam condensing into water and freezing into ice, so will *your* Word be made manifest.

Everything happens in the Now.
"Now is the day of salvation."
Now—now—now.

Chapter V

Fate — Destiny

"Born of woman ... is of few days ... filled with trouble. ... "

"Conceived in sin, born in iniquity."

Condemned from the start. There is little cheer to be found in looking forward, and less in looking backward. The vicious circle into which the human life has worked itself is nothing to contemplate with pleasure—such lovely and delightful things as, "As for man, his days are few and full of trouble." And all this beautiful picture is backed up by thousands of years of proof. It is also written in the palms of the hands; it is written in stars; it is written in names and numbers and even on the soles of the feet. Yes, it is a fact: as for man, his days are few and full of trouble. There is no escaping it.

Then comes one called Jesus, as much under a fixed destiny as we and yet understanding that within every man lies a power which is capable of setting aside human destiny.

Man has tried in every way to offset or escape his human fate, with small returns. He has tried a thousand and one "thought processes." Yet one of the first things Jesus discovered was that "taking thought" would accomplish nothing, and so He asked, "Who by taking thought can add one cubit to his stature?" And this same question is asked of you today. He further says, "If you cannot do that which is least (by taking thought), why will you try to do that which is greatest?" You answer this. Why will you persist in proclaiming yourself a follower of Jesus Christ and continue to subscribe to a thought-taking method?

Daily we see people trying to escape their human fate, so filled with trouble; but like the squirrel in a cage, they make much effort and get nowhere. The squirrel runs miles but goes only eighteen inches. In other words, he gets nowhere but back to where he started. So with the human thought: from the egg, the chicken; from the chicken, the egg.

Like the proverbial ostrich, man attempts to hide his eyes from evil. A thousand people have told me, "I do not actually believe in astrology, palmistry, or fortune-telling, and when they tell me anything evil, I refuse it. I accept only the good." But if they—"they"—can predict good, they can also predict evil, and if what they predict as good is to come to pass, so also what they find of evil must likewise come to pass. To deny the evil in this situation is like saying to mathematics, "The law of addition is all right, but I refuse the law of subtraction."

You have nothing to do with it. Your human fate in which you will function is fixed and sealed, as much so as your spiritual destiny. In the human fate, you will take the good, bad, and indifferent, whether you like it or not, as long as you function on the mental plane. You have discovered long ago that from the human standpoint it is much easier to do evil than to do good. Evil things happen so much more easily than the good ones. From the human standpoint, you have a great capacity to make mistakes, to do things wrong. In fact, you have to learn how to do things right because "as for man, his days are few and full of trouble."

Why? When you decided in the Garden of Eden to taste of the fruit of the Tree of Knowledge of Good and Evil, you set out to be a creator, disregarding the fact that the creation of the universe was perfect and finished. Nevertheless, you decided to create, and the world of thought-taking evil is the result of your work. Free will is still given to you. "Choose ye (not you and somebody else, but *you alone*) this day whom ye (you, not you and somebody else) will serve."

So this is where the so-called "taking-thought" business began. You felt you could change things by thinking about them, and even today people who profess to be teaching "Jesus Christ" are still instructing people to *think* right.

So inured to the tedium of fate has man become that he will blandly tell you that experiences, most always called problems, are good and that they help him to grow. Yet he is busy most of his life trying to escape the various "experiences" from which he claims he gets so much light. No wonder Jesus called the old human mind "a liar and the father of it." You have often heard a person in the so-called "Truth" saying of a condition he could not overcome, "This is good for me. I am getting a much-needed lesson." And so the outside of the platter is clean.

"I saw you under the fig tree" tells its story. Jesus could see through the whole pattern of human fate, just as He told the woman at the well all the things of her life. This is as possible to you as it was to Jesus, since you are told, "The works that I do ... and even greater." This gift of prophecy is part of your heritage; it is your prerogative to be able to see through or into any person, place, situation, or experience that is brought into your life. Can you accept this? It is not brought about by entering classes on mysticism or by developing classes of your own. We speak of spiritual prophecy—it is true, and not psychic claptrap.

The human mind has one capacity which is alike in all human beings—that of magnifying evil. The slightest suggestion of scandal or evil is magnified until it becomes a giant in the Philistine valley of life. Just as soon as a prediction is made regarding you, an onslaught of denials sets in. This merely accentuates the evil. The more one tries to avoid it, the surer he is of running into it. The human mind reverses the processes of the Divine and hence receives the magnifying of evil instead of the Lord within him, and his fears come upon him. The greatest intellects, with their highest findings, have been known to change their views and to deny everything they have said or found out to be true. No human being can say anything good about himself without prefacing it with some asinine remark such as, "I do not want to brag," and yet if he were speaking of Spirit, he could not brag.

We are awakening a little, perhaps. What do you think?

"Hold the thought" is another human teaching, wholly opposed to the teaching of Jesus Christ. He definitely said, "Take no thought." The point is well illustrated in the Hindu story of a man who went to a mystic and wanted to know how to become rich. He was told it was easy if he wanted to pay the price. So he was instructed in the ways of Consciousness, but just before the student went into his first meditation, the apparently mischievous holy man added: "But don't, for the slightest moment of your meditation, think of monkeys." The net result was that every time the student tried to meditate about riches, monkeys appeared, until finally he found himself constantly in a jungle of monkeys. Was Jesus right, or are you and some modern system of truth right, when you "take thought"?

Jesus knew that it was hopeless to fight against the fixed pattern of life. He also knew that He could of Himself do nothing. You, the reader, have probably already come to the same conclusion, having passed through a dozen or more "systems of truth" and as many or more teachers. Strange, too, since all claim to be followers of Jesus Christ.

If there is to be any escape from the human fate, which daily is causing you to do things you do not want to do ("When I would do good, I do evil"), it will be through a close adherence to the revelations of Jesus Christ and not through any man or organization — the assumption of His consciousness, the "Let that mind be in you which was also in Christ Jesus."

But first the differentiation between the mind of Jesus and the consciousness of Jesus Christ must be understood. The mind of Jesus was as human as your mind is and as filled with the human thought-taking limitations. He, as Jesus, could no more feed five thousand at a moment's notice than you could, for so long as He functioned on the Jesus (thought-taking) plane of life, it was utterly impossible to increase substance by giving away substance or to set aside time and space or to do a thousand and one other things that have not yet been told you.

There is no way to understand all this by human thought, yet when anything does come that sets aside human fate, immediately an attempt is made to explain it away. Failing in this, it is charged off to a mysterious thing called "a miracle" and the sooner forgotten the better.

Jesus came setting aside the fate of humankind. Every one of his "miracles" was proof of this.

He immediately broke the human fate atoms, substituting instead the Divine Destiny. The Divine Destiny of man is a heritage which he left when he departed (by request) from the Garden and wandered into a far country of belief and sub-creation. That Divine Destiny, however, has continued to function always, and every time the human man (Jesus) lifts himself up to this state, he immediately manifests what the human world has to call a demonstration. He is merely manifesting his true destiny, which is always wonderful.

The moment the human fate pattern is broken by the Jesus Christ Consciousness, the Divine Destiny is found functioning in all its glory, very much the same as a small opening in the clouds of the worst thunderstorm permits the sun to shine through. Whenever this happens, man exclaims, "I have made a demonstration," in the same silly manner as if he might say, "I have made the sun to shine," because he has made an opening through the clouds. The sun was always shining; his Divine Destiny was always functioning. Through the thunderstorm of his belief in good and evil, he has been able from time to time to elide, or blend with, his destiny.

Every time Jesus "went unto His Father," He was able to bring forth that which was functioning in his Divine Destiny at that moment. Hence, his eternal and uninterrupted success—and likewise yours. When you "return" to your Divine Destiny, you will automatically find yourself functioning on the plane of harmony, without the so-called necessary footsteps leading up to it. One moment of breaking through to this Divine Destiny causes man to function in a success which is humanly impossible.

Do you hear what I am saying to you? *It is wonderful* when you contemplate it, and that is why "it is done." Yes, Beloved, it is already done in your Divine Destiny. The reason you have such a desire for certain things is that they are at this instant functioning in your Divine Destiny.

All human prophecy, from whatsoever source, is broken up, dissolved, and put to flight with the coming of this Divine Destiny, and you—this funny little you—have the ability to "let" it come to pass, through the simple recognition of your Permanent Identity.

Created in the image and likeness of God, conceived in the mind of God, your beautiful Destiny is as marked and perfect as the path of the sun. It is the way of "helpless success." In other words, you can't help being a success. You bring with you from your Divine Destiny a capacity which is so definitely original, so different, so unique that you have no competition. You are a success because you cannot help it. You are a creature of Light in the universe of Life, and suddenly all the shadows of human fate disappear. You are freeborn. The old patterns are broken.

"When ye pray, enter the closet and shut the door." Prayer is a recognition of the presence of God within you and without you. There is no need to formulate words, for the moment you become conscious of this Presence within and without, all the evil with which you have been dealing, no matter of what intensity or power, no matter of what standing or duration, disintegrates, and the void of thought is filled with the substance of the Presence in the precise shape and form necessary to make Its omnipresent harmony manifest in a tangible form.

Entering this Presence is not by the way of thought. It is by pure assumption, which can be made only when you have come to "feel" the Presence. "You shall find Me when you feel after Me." In this Presence, in this place of the "feel," whatsoever you—not you and somebody, but you—tell the Father in secret shall be "called from the housetops." Immediately following this "telling" or perceiving of the finished thing, comes the challenge to you: "Believest thou this?"

If you can answer this in the affirmative without emotion, without fear, you can rise and go on your way, for the manifestation will take care of itself. "I have a way you know not of." There is no question about it because it is already done and finished. You have conceived it through the *sense-feel*, and no words are necessary to make it so.

It is a case of pure acceptance and has nothing to do with the old worn-out idea of concentration or visualization that says, "If you think hard enough or long enough, or picture a thing hard enough and long enough, you will bring it to pass." The best you can do with this system is to bring out clouds without rain, which are no good to you.

A man demonstrated a million dollars by visualizing a million dollars. He actually brought forth a million dollars worth of German Marks, which at one time had had a value of a million dollars but which now were worth only the paper they were printed on. The paper had not changed, but he had "clouds without rain."

Imagining "All that the Father hath is mine" will do nothing but drug you into a semi-comatose condition in which you will exist in a state of disillusion until you discover that at this very moment, regardless of what you have, you have all that your Father hath. Your Father is your recognition of the degree of God within you. Do you wonder, then, that Jesus admonished, "Launch out into deeper waters"?

There is no imagination in the life of Jesus if we interpret this word to mean credulity or childishness. When we assume such a state as "All that the Father hath is mine," it is an appropriation of "the substance of things hoped for" and "the evidence of things not seen" in the manifest world.

You are standing at the threshold of life. It is glorious. No matter where this finds you—in what condition, in what place, how much or how little you have had—it is all nothing. You are pushing back the curtains of a lovely new day. No matter with what swine you have consorted and what mud (of belief) you have on your garments, it is all nothing unless you persist in taking this past yardstick into the future.

You are born under the sign of God. "Call no man your Father … ." You are an aristocrat. No one has greater forebears than you, for you were created in the image and likeness of God; you partake of the nature of God. You have freed yourself from a thousand and one human beliefs to which you have been heir. You are directly under the influence and control of God, and in like manner you have been given control over everything in *your* universe— dominion over the stars, over the things on the earth, under the earth, in the sea, under the sea.

Note carefully how Jesus set aside human fate, broke patterns of years' standing, wiped out even karmic debts. Notice that the Magdalene wiped her slate clean with one "stepping-up" into the presence of her Divinity. She had arrived at a state of consciousness where she was being stoned to death by her own thought, which was embodied in men.

You will notice that she had been taken to the outer limits of her city (consciousness) and was being stoned. Unless she could go beyond that consciousness, she was to die—just as you, who have arrived at the walls or limits of a given state of consciousness of disease, fear, or poverty, must die in that city if you cannot get beyond it.

But suddenly she is saved from this destiny by the recognition of the Christ. All the evil thought embodied in men disappears. All the evidence of her past evil disappears. The harlot of human thought becomes the virgin of spirituality. The old disease-racked body suddenly becomes whole and fresh and immune. It becomes virgin. It is wonderful. We are speaking of the Christ-Consciousness. There are no words in which to put this, yet will you read between the lines and perceive.

Jesus, on the way to the cross, could easily have turned aside the fate which was facing Him, had He so desired. But He wanted to bring to us, definitely, that even the last enemy had no power and that eventually man would resurrect himself, even though his thought-body had been destroyed. He performed a surgical operation on the Roman centurion's ear, the like of which has never been heard or seen, even in the twentieth century. You seem to have overlooked this detail in your grief over Jesus. Well, ponder this a little too.

Jesus was able to stop the ongoing of human patterns set in motion by desire, neutralizing a whole life of evil and turning it into the pure fields of glorious Self-expression. You have set many evil things in motion. They are like hoops running down a hill, and they will continue with accelerated force until this force is spent—unless something knocks them over. That something that is to knock over these evil patterns of your human fate, many of which are now entirely out of your control, is the Jesus Christ Consciousness.

Do you begin to see why every knee will eventually bend at the name of Jesus, the one who gave us this beautiful revelation? Human thought and its results are fairly well-pictured in the story of the maniac in the tombs, playing with dead men's bones — playing with dead ideas in the graveyard, in the yesterday — and then suddenly he is in his right mind, sitting at the feet of the Master. Are you a maniac playing with the bones of dead men in the graveyard of yesterday, tortured by every fear and belief? Do you want to be in your right mind, sitting at the feet of the Master?

It is all as if we were suddenly coming into a new day of light and revelation, up through the slime of human thought into the place of pure unadulterated Presence. Everywhere, even in and through the most evil situations of the thought-taking world, comes this Light which disintegrates the congestion of human thought called evil.

Ye are born of Spirit. Ye are born again,
and you are beginning to
partake of your spiritual nature.

Chapter VI

Wist Ye Not?

Every question Jesus asked seemed to be full of surprise at the continued ignorance of man, even of his disciples. He had been with them three years, daily instructing them and guiding them into the new dimension, the Fatherhood degree of life. Yet they perpetually seemed to ask questions which belonged to the sonship degree. The business of Self-expression has been one of the most tortuous questions of all time, and so it came to Jesus.

"Wist ye not?" Jesus might well have said, "What—do you mean to tell me that after all this time, you do not know that I should be about my Father's business? Is it possible that you are still wondering about Life's expression? What are you asking questions about? Your place in the universe?"

All this surprise carries with it something deeper than the thought of the futility of words. It carries a deep, secret knowledge—that He knew that the disciples (who apparently *didn't* know that He should be about His Father's business) had innate possibilities of being about *their* Father's business.

When you begin to read the words of Jesus— I said *read*—you will discover revelation and inspiration. The surprise that is expressed in that one word, "What," is enough to fill you with wonder and with joy. Honestly, Jesus was surprised that man had not found out that his first and only consideration was to be about his Father's business, which is the business of life. When you begin to see this, even vaguely, you will not wonder any longer what your business is. You will discover it.

Pause a moment and see what this surprise question must mean to an awakening soul. Suddenly you move into the place of recognition (re-cognizing) the Fatherhood degree of life. It brings with it the extended vision which explains "Whereas I was blind, now I can see."

All the subtle revelation is between the lines of the message. All at once it is as if it were *shouted* to you, and suddenly within yourself you say, "Oh! Now I *see*"—see that by asking the question, Jesus has awakened in you the way *you*, the heir to this great heritage, have been mismanaging My affairs. He seems to be taking for granted that man already knows that such a state of affairs as the Father's business already exists, for He says to the most casual listener, "Go thou and do likewise." Not in the manner of doing something unusual, but in a perfectly normal, natural way, in the way of your own individual Christ-Consciousness.

Perhaps the easiest and the most difficult step in the ongoing of man is that of *assumption*, that something which must take place between the pigsty and the banquet of the fatted calf.

Assumption is when the congested human thought gives way to the flow of illumination that comes through the darkened senses of man.

This Fatherhood degree, wherein you begin to realize you are about *your Father's business*, is the point or place of contact with the universal cosmos. It is the *touch-in*, the point of contact, and is that which enables Jesus (John Smith) to do the things that he could not possibly do of himself because they are of another dimension. They are outside of all physical science.

To the man whose breath is in his nostrils, they come under the caption of supernatural, but they are only supernatural to the human mind. They are natural to the awakened Christ-Consciousness. "When ye be in the spirit, ye are no more under the curse of the law." The curse of the law is your human destiny, which will finally function in evil and death. Yet Jesus says, "The last enemy that shall be overcome is death." Do you believe this?

After this assumption has taken place in you, you begin a natural appropriation of the things and conditions which you formerly dreamed of bringing into manifestation. You begin to *take* your good. "Ask, and ye shall receive." There is no qualification whatsoever. "Knock, and it shall be opened unto you." Do you hear? "Seek, and it shall be found." Do you hear? It *shall be* opened unto you. You *shall* receive and you *shall* find.

Do you believe it? Is this possible? Or are you just hoping it will take place? It is so written in the law: "and it shall be opened unto you."

This "going about the Father's business" is the key to all manifestation. Thousands of people ask me about their place and their expression in the universe. Once they discover that they are about their Father's business, they will automatically find themselves expressing in harmony.

Remember that your Father is your concept of God. If it does not please you, if it is not enough, it is time that you contemplate the law—time that you "be still, and know that I am God" here, there, and everywhere. Contemplation of this God and His power will do more for you than ten thousand lessons in truth, affirmations of truth, or psychological ways and means that are given out to help you (and God) get into the kingdom of heaven.

Suppose you went into a bank and the President handed you a checkbook, saying that your signature would be honored for any amount. Could you take it? Could you sign? When you begin to *see*, you will find that your name (nature) will be honored for anything for which you can sign. "Ask whatsoever you will." It is so wonderful that it almost blinds one with illumination—this new day, this new dimension, this new revelation which Jesus so patiently tried to give to the world.

"The pure in heart shall see God." The pure in heart are those who sense-feel the reality of the Presence, become one with It and thereby bring It into manifestation. A "pure" mathematician would be one who was thoroughly conversant with the law of mathematics, and an "impure" one would be one who only half-believed in the same law. The higher mathematics goes the more abstract it becomes. At certain points it would seem completely to contradict its former statements, such as when it subtracts a greater number from a lesser, which, to the more ignorant thought, cannot possibly be done. And so with the manifestation of the higher laws of God—they confound and confuse with their simplicity the man "whose breath is in his nostrils."

"I shall ask my Father," as He has told me to "call upon me in the time of trouble, and I will answer you." Not maybe or perhaps, but *will* answer you. I shall not ask John Smith, a book, a teacher, a lecturer, or an organization. I shall ask my Father. Who will *you* ask?

Do you begin to see a difference between *radical reliance* on God and *a mere belief* in a tribal Jehovah? I shall ask my Father. Whom will you ask? "Let us go into the house (consciousness) of the Lord," the Lord of the universe. We suddenly, consciously enter in to Him. We live and move, breathe and have our being in Him, literally, actually—a Something that is more real than entering into any house built by man—and

He enters us, and lives and breathes and moves and has His being in us.

Do you begin to see the hookup between the within and the without? And why it is if you should "make your bed in hell," He would be there knocking at the door; and if you could *hear* (recognize) Him, He would come in and sup with you, thereby transmuting hell into heaven, for where heaven is, there is God.

Do you begin to see what it means to be about your Father's business? For the first time, you discover why you are here. Have you ever asked yourself, "What am I here for?" And have you ever come to the conclusion that your sojourn here wasn't of any great importance and that your mission seemed rather puerile? Once you conceive the fact that your Father's business is the business of Self-expression, you begin to experience new depths of understanding and new heights of revelation. A nice sense of the finished mystery takes possession of you—you are a revelator, no more a teacher or an expounder of the word.

What the world calls healing is merely the releasing of congested thought. The resurrection of the body might be likened to the picture on a camera plate. You know it is there because you took the picture. Though you cannot see it, you *know* it is there, and you can *prove* it by developing it. Now, you would never develop a plate unless you had good reason to believe that the picture was there, and so, in reality, you will never call upon God unless you are *sure* He is there. This perfect agreement between yourself and the Idea establishes the fact on earth. It is nothing you do—it is something you *do not* do. The moment you stop trying to hold up your universe and lean on Me, you will find yourself being sustained. It is strange and wonderful, yet it is so. Believest thou this? Answer me.

There is nothing fantastic about the use of this law. Jesus saw plainly that a child could do it but an adult could not, because an adult "knew" too much —had seen too many proofs and thus knew that it could not happen. "You must become as a little child." This is a *must*. It does not say to become childish, but it says to appropriate or discover within yourself that peculiar quality of accepting the Word without reservations. It is wonderful! It is glorious to contemplate the unselfishness of Jesus in trying to give mankind this wonderful revelation.

Such a change will come over your business affairs, the moment you consistently enter every transaction with the consciousness that you are "about your Father's business," that both you and your client will be surprised at what takes place. There is so much light in this consciousness of the Father's business that no matter how humanly ignorant you may be, you are protected by this light from any unintentional dishonesty. You cannot fall into any trap that is dug for you, but the Light through you can cause the one who set the trap to step into it himself.

"Wist ye not?" Do you sense all the wonder of why you, in the Father degree, cannot now be out of alignment with the perfect, eternal harmony of life? From this moment on, you will begin to perform many things and experience many glories that are not spoken of in books. You will transmute, you will change anything that must be changed or transmuted. In the relative way of thinking, man goes from problem to problem. But in the Fatherhood degree, you go "from glory to glory," that is, from illumination to illumination.

On your path of Divine Destiny are so many things you have never thought of that you are in a constant state of delight and wonder.

> The blessings are as the sands of the sea. So I ask you, "What! Wist ye not that I must be about my Father's business?" Do you hear?

Chapter VII

No Thought

The air inside of a vase takes the shape of the vase automatically. If it were possible to withdraw the air entirely and create a vacuum, a perfect vacuum, the vase would collapse. The pressure of the air on the outside would be too great to be withstood.

Applying this illustration to your everyday problem, take your thought away from or out of a problem, and it will automatically collapse, to be "absent from the body" (the embodiment of evil) and present with the law.

All evil is the product of thought and is sustained by it. It has no other cause. It is not self-creative or self-sustained; it must be fed and fanned into a flame by thought. Thus, the mere spread of gossip has been fanned into a veritable forest fire of manifestation, which has sometimes ended in war, and this too many times caused by a wholly untrue report. Thus, we see why Jesus repeatedly warned against the evil of "taking thought."

The devil was supposed to have been created by "walking up and down, and to and fro." We are all familiar with the old adage, "Mischief finds some work for idle hands to do." But the hands will not do anything evil unless thought has first conjured up a picture of evil for them to perform. Taking away the thought, or being "absent from the body," might be likened to deflating a balloon. This monstrous shape that appears so formidable crumples to nothing when it is deprived of its gas. And while all illustrations are inadequate to express God in any sense of the word, yet by parables and illustrations are we able to grasp somewhat the action of God. "Out of mind, out of body." It is perfectly amazing how far-reaching this thing is.

It follows quite naturally that if you are to take the life-substance away from a given situation, you cannot first add to the appearances of this evil by judging from the appearances. Everything you recognize in your thought-world as true can bring out its manifestation, just the same as when you perceive a true state in consciousness it reveals the "finished mystery."

The command "judge not from appearances" is given to you not so much as a restriction but rather as very powerful instruction on how to escape evil. The more you examine the nature of evil the more real it becomes. A pin scratch on a day laborer and a pin scratch on a movie star are two entirely different things as far as results are concerned (though the movie star's father may have been a day laborer.) Now, are you the day laborer, or are you the movie star, symbolically speaking? "Awake thou that sleepest, and Christ shall give thee light." This is not an oft-repeated command—it is a revelation, when you finally *hear* it. You will awaken to a new level and will certainly exclaim to yourself, "Whereas before I was blind, *now* I can see."

When we speak of human thought, it really should be called mis-thought, for in reality, real thought comes only from Consciousness. It is the emanation of light and understanding, at no time creative but always revealing, whereas human thought is the creator and sustainer of all evil. That is why it is possible to disintegrate human thought patterns.

I do not need to list a thousand and one incidents where actual disease and untoward conditions have been made manifest, through thought-taking, out of absolutely nothing. Perhaps one of the most pertinent illustrations is that of the man who died of cholera because he was told he had been exposed to it, when not a single instance of cholera had ever been heard of in that vicinity. Perhaps there is something to the phrase, "I am *catching* a cold." What do you mean, "catching"?

Judging righteous judgment, or taking the thought away from the body, will devitalize the thought-power, thereby automatically eliminating the effect of sin, disease, lack. Sometimes this can be done instantly; the thread of thought can be snapped so quickly that the manifestation disappears like magic.

Taking your attention away from the so-called evil does not mean hiding your eyes from appearances and violently declaring against evil. You may stand open-eyed before it and devitalize it by the presence of your newly-awakened God-power. "You must decrease, I must increase" literally takes place as you begin to understand how the thought of Jesus merges into the consciousness of Christ.

Confronted with the situation of five thousand hungry people all clamoring for bread, He apparently was faced with a real problem. We see He "lifted his eyes to heaven"—not somewhere up in the air but to his Christ-Consciousness—where He instantly recognized that the picture of evil formed by thought had nothing to sustain it. No wonder He could give thanks. It did not make any difference what the human mind said was true. The moment the thought was broken, the manifestation disappeared.

Do you begin to see why evil is not made more real actually by the thoughts of five thousand people? Because "one with God is a majority." In other words, *one* who takes his attention away from thought and places it in the Christ-Consciousness, his Perfect Identity, is more powerful than thousands who are trusting in the force of evil.

A parasite dies automatically the moment the sap or substance upon which it lives is cut off. All human problems are parasites that through thought-taking apparently have grown on the life of man. Very much as barnacles on a ship are no part of the ship, so evil and its manifestation are no part of man. Claim your heritage. Begin to magnify the Lord within. Begin to identify yourself with your Permanent Identity. "Look unto me, all ye ends of the earth, and be ye saved."

A ship that is covered with barnacles eventually will sink unless they are removed. Its speed is impeded; the strain on the engines is greater as this mass of evil enlarges. There are two ways of removing barnacles from ships. One is the dry dock, where men labor with steam drills and other instruments to chisel away this hard formation. The other is by running the ship into fresh water docks, where the barnacles automatically drop off.

There are two ways of getting rid of evil in your life—one by working with the outside, trying to overcome appearances which you call real, which is an almost hopeless task, and the other is by running the thought-laden mind into the unchanging, pure Consciousness of Spirit. So many unknown conditions and problems will drop out of your life the moment you make your contact with your Divinity. Magnify the Lord within you. Praise His holy name.

Once you have taken your attention from evil, thereby shutting off the supply of thought-substance, the appearance of evil will disintegrate, and the place thereof will be no more. The breath of God will blow the vanishing particles into oblivion. "The former things are passed away; they shall not be remembered, nor come into mind anymore." Whatever apparently resists this power is moved out of the way, be it person, place, or thing. The blessing of the Lord, descending on such resisting appearances, is a consuming fire. Fear not. Once you have released it in thought, any apparent reality of evil, no matter how time-honored, is consumed. It is written in the law, "The former things shall pass away ... ." They "shall not be remembered (do you hear?), nor come into mind any more."

If this law is to be carried out effectively—and it is—no (not any) person, place, or remembrance of the thing can stand in the way of the ongoing of God. The stone-casters who have come out against you will suddenly flee, confounded with a sudden spasm of fear, from a power against which they cannot stand—confounded, turned awry, twisted, and babbling like chattering monkeys in the jungle. All the scandal-mongers and gossipers shall be sent into the wilderness to eat their own words. Stand and see the holy fires consume the burnt offering. And again we hear, "Only speak the word." Think of it. *You* have been given this power. "Search the scriptures, for in them ye think ye have eternal life."

Stand and see the salvation of the Lord and thrill in the knowledge of His presence. "Who is so great a God as our God?" "Is anything hard to me?" You answer that one. If you feel that there is anything hard for God to do or that your problem is difficult for Him, then you must pray the prayer which will change this belief, the prayer of contemplation: "Be still, and know that I am God."

This is contemplation of the Power. The more you contemplate it, the more you begin to actually sense-feel Omnipotence and the more your so-called problem dwindles in importance. Remember, God transcends everything, no matter from what source or belief. Time means nothing to this Presence. Time is only a measure of evil made by man. "His days are few and full of trouble." Yet in the mind of God, "a thousand years may be as a day," or if more time is needed, a day may be as a thousand years.

Do you begin to see somewhat how an understanding of the power of God can stretch or telescope the human belief of time? This is an important thing for you to know in the event it ever has to be done. Jesus did it all the time. He "passed through the crowd," was "instantly on the other side of the lake." Never does the man who understands the law attempt to prove it. This very attempting to prove it shows that he does not believe in it. Although you have been silent all night, you do not *attempt* to speak English in the morning when you arise—you just speak it. You do not *try* to speak it. Why?

Finally we begin to see that the manifestation of God-power in your life is not some trick of a twentieth century religion but a natural condition which functions automatically and in its functioning destroys evil pictures of human thought. At no time is it fighting or *trying* to overcome them any more than you are trying to speak English. You only try to speak English when you do not know English. You only *try* to demonstrate God when you do not actually *know* God; yet sometimes in both instances you are able to make yourself understood.

It makes no difference how mortal mind is inconvenienced, how its beliefs are set aside or overturned, how its best-established laws are made as nothing. It makes no difference whether it ever has happened before or ever will happen again. Nothing the human mind can say or think amounts to anything when it comes to the expression of the God-power.

Have you noticed that when a thing cannot be explained or handled it is called an act of God? This is fastened onto most of the evil situations which man cannot explain. The sharp surplus of evil thought eventually collects itself and manifests itself in evils over which man himself has no control. The old Adam hiding again in the garden from his own evil explains, "I was naked and I was afraid." So the human mind, when it has set into motion its evil, is afraid and takes refuge in the explanation, "This is an act of God," in a further attempt to make the Divinity a god of good and evil.

All sorts of fantastic things are mentioned in the Bible. "Yon mountain" and "yon sycamore tree" and many other things are told to do and perform things wholly outside their nature. We are not talking about any human power or its limitations. We are speaking of divine power, and it clearly states, "Nothing (not a single thing) is impossible to God." Do you know of something that is? If not, you probably know someone who does. In such case, you or he does not believe in God. You believe in a man-made God, a God of limitations, and naturally your results must be in accordance with these limitations.

"There is a reason for the hope that is within us," and there is a deep sense of joy welling up within you as you begin to know that the hellish thing or condition which has been filling your life and body with fear and sickness and all sorts of untoward conditions is at last beginning to quake with the fear of this "terrible" power of the Lord, "for the Lord Omnipotent reigneth."

Jesus always ascended to the place of the Father. To ascend, in this sense of the word, does not mean to go up but is merely an expression of changing the thought to Consciousness. There, in that ascended place, He rediscovered the fact that God controlled all planes of manifestation — mineral, vegetable, animal — and that to be one with this power was to manifest that same control if called upon to do so.

It checks perfectly with your so-called birth certificate — "born of God," "made in the image and likeness of God," "given dominion over everything on the earth, in the earth, and over the earth." Claiming this birthright brings you into a wonderful inheritance. There are many wonderful things interpolated for you—words of power, unseen until the eyes are opened; secrets, deep mystical revelations; and the keys to the kingdom of heaven.

No wonder you are admonished to search the scriptures. Did you ever hear this quotation: "Thus far, and no farther"? I am asking you if you ever heard it or if you know what it means, as far as you are concerned and in the event you should ever have to use it. Remembering all the while that you are not studying a new system of religion but are having revealed to you Life, what you formerly called demonstration will immediately take place as a perfectly natural result of a different cause. There is nothing exciting or emotional in this appearance. Even the winds and waves obeyed Him.

Jesus, without His Father-Consciousness, had no more power than you have, and He admitted this. You can know the truth mentally from now until the end of time, and nothing will happen. And so with Jesus. He could of Himself do nothing; His conduct differed from ours in that He never *tried* to do anything. He did not waste time taking thought about things or trying to change them but immediately ascended to the place of his Father-Consciousness. He knew full well that nothing could come from taking thought except "clouds without rain." You have probably seen someone, working with some system of psychology or metaphysics, bring out an oversized manifestation with nothing to support it and have seen that same apparently beautiful manifestation collapse and disappear as a mirage in the desert.

Again I repeat: thought is the creator of evil and the sustainer of evil. Watch! From Consciousness emanates all real thought, or light, but neither the human nor this light-thought is a creator.

For instance, suppose a person tells you about a friend. Immediately your human thought builds up a picture of this person in infinite detail, and your thought elaborates on the subject either for good or evil, according to what you have been told. When one day you come in contact with the person, your entire picture is completely shattered because it never did exist as a reality; but from the moment you saw the person, you had a consciousness of him, and certain thoughts began to form or emanate from this consciousness. The same thing is true of the picture of disease and evil in your life. You have been told since childhood about certain evil things, and not until you come into the consciousness of Life are these evil pictures disintegrated.

Have you remarked what an apparent dearth there is of so-called healings and demonstrations, yet years ago they seemed to be very general? You hear people today in many organizations giving testimonies about things that happened twenty years ago. Why?

The reason is that after the "signs" have been given, you are either moving into the place of manifestation or you are with the dog, so unlovely, who does such an unlovely thing as to "return to his vomit"—go back to his old beliefs; or you are the dog under the table eating the crumbs instead of being the host at the banquet table of life.

If you are still "taking thought," you are still looking for signs and wonders. "Come out from among them and be ye separate." The signs will follow; they do not precede. You understand this, don't you?—even while you are saying in the next breath, "Before they ask, I will answer." In your spiritual revelation, you find not a *single* contradiction in the law of God.

As human thought is the substance of all evil so is cosmic Power the "substance of all things hoped for, the evidence of things not seen." It is wonderful when you get the proper perspective on the whole. Suddenly you will "put up your sword," stop fighting evil problems and appearances, and begin to call upon God in the true sense of the word. Then will you know that "as a thief in the night" this Power has appeared and cleared the whole ground of its miasma of evil, be this evil person, place, or thing. It is, as I said, confounded, dumbfounded, confused, turned around, driven into a fury of its own mentality from which there is no escape. Stand and see. It is wonderful!

The walls of the city of Jericho crumbled away into a cloud of dust. Today a thin line of yellow-green banana trees marks the spot "where the body lies." You may go in and come out of Jericho in a thousand places; there is no further obstruction. Your Jericho, or desire, may be surrounded by a wall, either figuratively or actually, as formidable as that which was around the city of Jericho. But there comes a moment in your understanding and revelation when the trump sounds and the walls become a cloud of dust, swept away into oblivion.

Never born, never dying, you are being freed from the barnacles of thought.

> "Then lifted he his eyes unto heaven and said, Thank you, Father." And then He broke the bread and fed five thousand, against the most cherished beliefs that the human thoughts of those five thousand knew to be true. And again I admonish you, "Take no thought."

Chapter VIII

Natural and Supernatural

Everything that has to do with Spirit has been labeled supernatural. Therefore, it has been entirely out of the reach of the so-called natural man. Yet things that your forebears thought supernatural are today perfectly natural. Formerly, man thought that lightning was an evil power with which God punished evildoers. Today a three-year-old child handles lightning with impunity; and though only vaguely understood, it now seems quite natural to press a button or turn a switch and cause it to do all sorts of wonderful things.

Jesus came with a conscious knowledge that the so-called supernatural law, which apparently had been used only to work "miracles," was a perfectly *natural* capacity of the awakened man. In other words, He knew that within man lay this Christ-Consciousness, this Permanent Identity, this Father within, which was the point of contact between God and man. The moment He ascended to this Consciousness, He was able to release this so-called supernatural power with the same ease that a child could flood a skyscraper with light by merely throwing a small switch.

Time and space are virtually eliminated by the use of electricity. A man can throw a switch in Washington, D. C., and flood with light an exposition on the West Coast. Time and distance are nothing to him. He does not have to make a bigger effort because he is not in the proximity of the fair; he does not have to work himself up emotionally; he merely has to pull the switch. And so is it with the God-power, only more so; and that is why your word, when spoken in Washington, D. C., is picked up and made manifest in China just as easily as if the person affected were in the same room. We have long ceased to wonder at the thousand and one miraculous things performed by electricity, because it has become a natural thing, an automatic thing; and this is the precise altitude at which Jesus functioned. He found the supernatural natural.

We know now perfectly well that the radio might well have been used in Jesus' time as far as the principle is concerned. No one recognized it, so it was not manifest. It is the same with all spiritual power. Until it is recognized and thereby given a channel of expression, it remains invisible.

In the Bible there are dozens of instances of the prophets hearing voices from afar at odd and sundry times. Today, through the use of radio, this does not cause even a flurry of emotion; you take it as a perfectly natural thing. Things that were denounced as rank heresy in former ages are found to be indispensable aids in the present time.

So thoroughly familiar with the law was Jesus that many of his sayings are fraught with surprise at the lack of comprehension. In the case of Lazarus, He actually wept when He was told that he had died. Having been so long in the household of Lazarus, explaining this supernatural, natural law, He could scarcely believe that such gross ignorance of it was still there. Martha even said to Him, "Lord, if you had been here, our brother would not have died," showing that she looked upon Jesus as a worker of miracles and utterly failed to understand His teachings, which said, "Go thou and do likewise," indicating that He recognized this power as the prerogative of every man. We, therefore, are not taking anything from the glory of Jesus when we make the assumption of this God-Self in us; rather, we are actually carrying out His plan.

The human mind is loathe to part with the mysterious, and so we find it arguing even against the teaching of Jesus, after having had many magnificent proofs. Again we return to the Lazarus situation. Jesus said, "He is asleep; I go to awaken him." Did they believe it? Even when said by Jesus? They did not, but they immediately began to explain all the old human laws that had set in which would make this utterly impossible. "He has been dead four days; the body is putrefying; it is impossible." And so the old human thought denied its God again and found something *impossible*, while in the next breath it would be affirming, "All things are possible to God."

Do you believe? Mary and Martha didn't, even when they were told by Jesus Himself. In other words, could you possibly take your good if it came to you, or do you know also that he has been dead four days—with plenty of evidence to back it up? In other words, do you *believe?* You *think,* yes, but when faced with the actual impossible situation, you are looking for a miracle. You are not anticipating any natural-supernatural manifestation.

Nothing can be done with the teachings of Jesus until He is understood to be a truthsayer and not a liar and until the assumption is made that "as he is, so are we, in this present world." Dare you to make this assumption—you poor, downtrodden worm of the dust or you arrogant peacock, strutting your importance and fame in your make-believe world? Jesus asked always, "Believest thou that I am able to do this?" And you must answer for yourself.

Just as a man who handles electricity intelligently and causes it to do all sorts of fantastic and interesting things is not doing a supernatural thing, so a man who becomes conscious of his God-Self is not doing a supernatural thing, because whatever he does at that elevation is perfectly natural, no matter how it may mystify the man "whose breath is in his nostrils."

"Nothing is impossible to Me" is a law as natural and as probable to the consciousness which enters into a recognition of its true Identity as any natural law is to the so-called natural man. To five thousand people, Jesus showed the law of precipitation as a natural thing. He knew that when a man was hungry he should be able to eat because, in reality, he was fed spiritually and clothed spiritually; but until man *knew* this, he came under the so-called natural law, which said he should earn his living by the sweat of his brow.

It is wonderful when you, the reader, discover that you are fed and clothed spiritually. It means just this—that you will never want again. "Man shall not live by bread alone, but by every word that proceedeth out of the mouth of God." Do you begin to see why you are told to take the journey without thought of the purse, the scrip, the robe?

Notice the surprise of Jesus when many of the five thousand who were with Him when He showed them the law of precipitation came again and asked Him for bread. His answer to them is one of the greatest revelations in all of the scriptures: "You seek me after the loaves and fishes, and not the miracle (law)," showing clearly that He had fully expected them to understand the naturalness of His bringing forth that substance.

It is perfectly amazing when we see what this man Jesus was attempting to give to the world, yet most of us, like these gluttonous onlookers, want demonstrations instead of understanding and revelation. It is recorded in one place that even His disciples asked for bread after they had seen the law (had experienced the miracle of the loaves and fishes). Do you understand now why the "Awake thou that sleepest, and Christ shall give thee light" is so important? It says, "Awake, open your eyes." Jesus was standing before a group of people who apparently were physically awake, yet He said, "Ye have eyes and see not, and ears and hear not, lest it should enter into your hearts."

You are not told to argue with the Power. If you want fine clothes, you are told how to get them very easily; but I find nothing in the law which says, "Sit down and think about a red hat and see a red hat and handle a red hat, and maybe you will get a red hat." More than likely, it will not go with anything you have to wear, and by the time you bring out a red dress to go with it, the red hat is worn out; and by the time you get another, red is out of date—and so the old squirrel cage process of taking thought goes on. It never goes anywhere except where it started. Yet you are told how to clothe yourself beautifully, if necessary, by simply considering the lilies.

It seems rather silly, doesn't it? Child's play— or maybe you think it is horseplay—and that is all it is on the human, thought-taking plane. *Looking* at lilies, or even considering them, will get you nowhere until you understand what is back of the command. "They toil not, they spin not, they gather not into barns, and yet Solomon in all his glory was not arrayed like these." Why? It is wonderful when you begin to see the natural-supernatural law that is functioning here, and if a lily can fulfill its mission so beautifully and so naturally, even to the envy of a Solomon, how much more should you, "Oh ye of little faith!"

When man begins to see the naturalness of the spiritual law, he will also see that anything he asks for in that nature will be perfectly natural to him and not supernatural. When you ask for anything in the name, that is, merely the letters and phonetics of the name, nothing takes place; but when you ask in the name-nature, things happen. Just as when you sign your name to a check—your name is no good unless you have the *nature* to do it, and then it produces results.

There were many things which Jesus said He could not tell us because of our unbelief. In fact, it has been most difficult for most of us even to accept as true the things that He did tell us. He did not say He would not tell us these wonderful new laws and revelations but that He could not at that time because we would not believe in them as natural. So there is something wonderful awaiting you when you finally enter into your closet and shut your door. It seems to me that the time has just about come for us to know some of these higher things so that we may "go through," even though "ten thousand fall at our right hand." Do you understand what I am talking about? You are "hid with Christ in God."

This all brings us to a lovely sense of the Now, where we actually begin to speak in the present tense and the first person and, in some degree at least, begin to experience the kingdom here at hand and the naturalness of a so-called supernatural law. Amazing things are said to us—they almost take our breath away when we hear and see them—such as, "Go in and possess the land." Hadn't you better go back and read that one over again, that "Go in and possess the land?" Do you hear it? Go in and possess the Consciousness, without asking permission of anybody for anything. Do you hear? Do you believe?

It is for this that a man will "sell all" and "buy the pearl of great price." He will get rid of all his beliefs in leaders, books, organizations and will follow after the Christ. He is then through with the idea that someone is coming who will show forth a lot of new miracles. He will glimpse, at least faintly, the fact that he is to be the miracle worker as far as *his* life is concerned. He must make this assumption. He must find it natural to do the supernatural, and gradually he will find himself doing many things which he formerly thought were miracles but which now seem quite natural. The mystery of godliness is its simplicity.

As you begin to see how natural this super-natural law is, you will see that fear of life is absorbed into a reverence of this glorious power made so plain to us by Jesus, just as on the human plane, fear of lightning was transmuted into a respect for the laws of electricity. "The fear of the Lord is the beginning of wisdom." Do you hear? The reverence for this law which is to operate through your temple-body into manifestation is absolutely necessary. It is too precious to be discussed with the man "whose breath is in his nostrils" and who is still looking for signs and wonders. The coal of fire is placed on your lips, and you will not "cast that which is holy to the dogs."

As modern business debunks false methods, so the coming of Jesus takes away all mysteries surrounding life, bringing supernatural law (which has seemed to be peculiar to a group of religious characters and prophets) down to a natural basis so that the man in the street can operate it with the ease of a child.

It is so amazing when you think that all a man must do to see this glorious power in manifestation is to *believe!*

Chapter IX

Wars and Rumors of Wars

War at its most terrific is actually the result of one man's thoughts multiplied by millions of others. It is possible only by the agreement we make with it. Millions agree that inharmony is the order of the day, and they experience all sorts of evil which terminates in death and destruction. What you accept is yours and comes to pass regardless of what anyone declares. What you find to be true within yourself takes place in the without. A stream of consciousness passing through your "John Smith" is colored by what your individual mind accepts as true. Hence, "one man's meat is another man's poison." It is wonderful when you begin to see that only what you accept as real and true can be true to you *and only that to which you give power can have power over you.*

At first, your human intellect is affronted and offended with such a statement and would recite hundreds of incidents to prove that it is not so. You know many things have happened to you that you did not think of or accept as real and true; but *nothing can take place in your human life that has not been accepted by you as true at some time or other.*

War is a man-made thing; its foundation is greed and hatred. If he cannot go to war, man *can* bring war to himself; and if he is too fearful, he may bring it into his own home. Two women working in a field in Florida were decapitated by an airplane. Few worse things could have happened to anyone in the war, yet they were thousands of miles from any battlefront.

Do you begin to see how it is that you have been making your own life and that something must be done to offset this haphazard process? Despite all the inventions of modern civilization, thousands of years seem to have been entirely wasted and the simplest teachings of Jesus Christ still not understood.

Today we are being mesmerized by floods of words. We need to see and hear *aright*. We become afraid of everything that man says, for tomorrow he changes. There is a good deal of praying that goes on, praying for victory or a nation or a person, regardless of the fact that God is no respecter of persons or nations (even though many people may imagine He is of English extraction). Praying for relief from expected evil will give us nothing, for the human intellect has too much proof of what it has either seen or heard of evil to throw it off so easily.

War is a natural function of human thought and goes on eternally between nations and even between members of a family. Until it puts on Christ, the

Fatherhood degree, the human consciousness will continue its way, despite the revelation, "Behold, what manner of love the Father has bestowed upon us." Do you see that it *already* has been bestowed upon us, that it is not a future salvation we are speaking of? Do you see that this love already has been bestowed on us now and here? It is only an abstract idea until we begin to experience it through this Christ-Consciousness. "Love never fails." Never is a long time, and so it is the spiritual love that clears the way for manifestation.

In the midst of all the fury of mortal mind, you abide in the City of Refuge prepared for you, remembering all the while that all this is just another appearance from which you must not judge. God is there when you are conscious of Him, no matter what the appearances. Remember also that if you make your bed in hell, there am *I* and that where *I* am, there is heaven. "The water shall not quench thee, neither shall the fire burn thee." You are "hid with Christ in God." It is well.

And also comes the wonderful speaking of the Word from behind the lines to those in the trenches or on the sea. Knowing now, as you do, the power of the Word and that *I* am here, there, and everywhere, your *Word* is *instantly* with that one absent from you in the physical, and it surrounds him with a panoply of love and fearlessness and protection through which no device of man can or will pass. All this is

I Came

so sacred and holy it is almost profaned by putting it on paper, because of the unbelief of many.

The lines of communication between you and the one out there are perfectly established. Jesus saw everything that the woman under the fig tree had done. There is the power to *see*, when you accept it and when you *believe* in the word of God. Are you beginning to see what the radical reliance on God has in store for you? It opens up the doors to your senses, extending them into the beyond and giving you the only information worthwhile.

"I am with you always, even unto the end" of this human fury. *I* will hold your right hand, saying unto you, "Fear not." This can take place literally as well as symbolically if you are prepared to accept it as true. "My sheep hear my voice." Do *you* hear?

If there is no war in your consciousness, there is no war in manifestation as far as you are concerned. You may move through the pictures of it all, but only that which is in your consciousness can actually take place. There is no fear in your consciousness; therefore, there is nothing to make you afraid on the outer, though you move through a thousand manifestations of so-called evil.

Watch, and do not commit war within the borders of your own home. A woman recently committed suicide when she read of the slaughter of three hundred innocents; she couldn't stand it. Next morning the report was corrected; only three had been killed. Thought is capable of all evil, and it can act from a supposed cause just as well as a real one. Watch—if there is no war in your heart, there can be none in your world.

When Peter was put into prison, he sang until the walls gave way. Not once did he recognize the appearances as something real, and those appearances which depended on the support of his thought gave way. It took an earthquake to do it, but that is nothing. The jailers ran, and finally they invited Peter to come out—invited the very one they had thrown into prison. "I have a way ye know not of." It is wonderful!

The great cosmic Ring of Fire around the whole world is today cleansing it of much of its evil. Everything that does not belong here will be purified by this fire, as will every evil place and condition, and these fires will not abate until the last bit of dross is burned up and the kingdom of heaven is established on earth.

Jesus was a truthsayer, and He said, "This is the kingdom of heaven," here and now, and everything that is making it a hell must and will be purified out of this existence by the cosmic cleansing fires.

The victory is not yours but God's. You are merely a temple of the living God where this victory may be made manifest. You can do what you are called upon to do, for you are led by the Spirit. And instead of the baptism of fire, you shall have the baptism of glory. You will stand in the downpour of Light and revelation and exclaim, "My

105

Lord and my God." You have on the armor of righteousness and the breastplate of Love through which no bullet can penetrate. It is wonderful—and so it is.

Remember always that the moment the war-thought is killed out of the minds of men, at that moment the physical slaughter will cease, and what is true of a nation is true an individual.

The Hebrew children passed through fire without any ill effects; yea, not even the smell of fire was upon their garments. How will you pass through this fire of human emotion when the whole world is burning with hatred, greed, and the lust for power? Will you come out with the smell or the stink (to put it in more plebeian words) of fire or war on your garments? Remembering that the men who built that fire were burned to death, isn't it time for you to see that even though you walk through the fire it will not burn you, nor will it leave the smell of fire on your garments?

Do you begin to see the difference in it all? You are in a New Day, and you have taken the new road or path into the kingdom of Here and Now; and the moment you fully conceive this, you will go through the fire of experiences that may be about you, without the smell of fire on your garments.

There is no argument. Either you see and believe or you make certain reservations. If you make reservations about the God-power, you will come under the laws of a limited power. If you find any man whom you consider more powerful than God and more omniscient in his wisdom, then you should worship that man, believing that if every mortal man is a truthsayer, then Jesus Christ is a liar! Argument lifts its hydra head and protests with, "Yes, I know, but ... "

Which do you choose?

The "call upon me, and I will answer you," is no more true in the days of no war than it is true in the days of total war. Do you begin to see that all the laws of Truth you have been prating about during the years of so-called peace are just as true now as then, or else they were never true?

If you believed in protection when the world was at peace, how much more should you "enlarge the borders of your tent" *now* and see that this very sense of protection reaches out over the entire world. And though your loved ones may be in the midst of the fury of battle, still shall My hand lead them—not so much as a matter of demonstration but just because appearances of which you have talked so long are still appearances, no matter of what intensity they may be.

It is all a more glorious opportunity to "stand ye still, and see the salvation of the Lord," to see and to know that what you have talked about in so-called times of peace is just as real and true in so-called times of war. For the warfare is not ours but God's.

Do you begin to understand that this confusion which has enveloped the entire *thinking* world is just an enlarged opportunity for you to make good in your belief in God? Now you are getting a real chance to see whether or not you believe in God.

Remember what the answer was to the question of the disciples when they returned in the evening and saw that the fig tree had been withered away: "Lord, how could these things be?" In other words, How in the world could a fig tree which was perfectly healthy and normal, in full foliage this morning, be now (a few hours later) a withered thing? Do you recall the answer—and what it carries with it?

Do you recall the answer? It is so simple that it is almost tragic. Jesus did not qualify it this time with tears or surprise. He said simply, "Have faith in God," and in that simple, unqualified statement, He gave the key to the kingdom of Power here and now.

Well, nearly everybody who reads those wonderful words says within himself, "I have faith in God—but why is it that my problem does not work out? How is it that my fig tree, which flourishes in all its glorious evil, does not wither?" And the very question answers itself. It is plain that the average person thinks the faith that is required is a sickly belief that just believes in God as you believe in a lucky charm or a formula or an affirmation or a "hunch."

The cosmic fires which are lighted will burn out the dross. This time, the kingdom of heaven here on earth is to be established. We are beginning to see that the immaculate conception is to be established on earth. Unless we believe in this, we might just as well "return to our vomit" of yesterday's findings and believe in what the eye sees and the ear hears, in spite of the rebuke, "Ye have eyes, and see not; and ears, and hear not ... ."

Do you begin to see why it is that the truth is individual and not collective? A nurse and a doctor move amid thousands of cases of malignant disease without becoming infected. Why? You say they are protected; they have taken certain precautions and so are all right. You begin to see, when you understand the truth of your Permanent Identity, that you too are protected and that you too have taken certain precautions and that it is all right. You are beginning to see that you are moving through pictures which in a few years will give forth many new and startling revelations as to cause and effect. So it is time that you appropriated your good and began to function in the New Day of Life.

And so the "wars and rumors of wars" pass along. They have been since the beginning of time and at all times began with the human thought-taking, which thought it could create a better world than God had created. Into this whole fiasco came Jesus Christ, telling of the kingdom of heaven here and now. But the theologians of that day would not tolerate the loss of their prerogatives, and so they crucified him and again tried to return man to the belief in "an eye for an eye, and a tooth for a tooth"—and many are so caught with the idea that they actually fall again into the pre-Christ teaching. But after the smoke of battle has cleared away, then will come again the illumination that Jesus was a truthsayer and every mortal man "a liar and the father of lies."

Chapter X

Why Do You Say Possibly?

And Jesus said to the father of the possessed child, How long has he been like this? And the father answered, From a little child ... but if you possibly can, have compassion on us, help us. And Jesus answered and said, Why do you say possibly?

Does that question mean anything to you? Do you hear or see anything in the answer? Something which should make your heart leap with joy? The perpetual surprise expressed by Jesus that people still doubted the power of the Presence to set aside the congealed human thought—"Why do you say *possibly?*"

It is terrific when you stop for a moment and contemplate this answer of Jesus. Just reading it over does nothing. Pause a moment and let it penetrate through that darkened state of mentality which continually is wondering whether or not the power "can possibly" heal its condition. Why do you say *possibly?*

Isn't it thrilling? More and more we enter into a secret conspiracy with Jesus against the "set" condition in our lives, that peculiar pet problem which has been there so long, "since he was a child," as it were. Suddenly it is as though you actually heard the voice of Jesus speaking to you about your "maniac" child—the human mind—and standing directly in front of you, asking you that same question, "Why do you say *possibly*?" God is the doer of the impossible, and that cannot be measured or handled with the human thought, for it cannot glimpse what the impossible is.

Do you see why Jesus frequently left the limited carpenter-consciousness and entered into the Permanent Identity and became one with God? Do you begin to understand what He meant when He said, "I will ask my Father," and the Father, hearing in secret, shall "declare it (I said *shall*) from the housetops." Not *maybe* or *perhaps* what you tell the Father—*whatsoever* you can find in this God-power in secret shall be declared from the housetops of manifestation.

When a thing becomes "impossible," it is then possible to God. If it is impossible to you, it is because you have utilized every bit of human wisdom you have in an attempt to move it, and at last you have come to the extremity of human thought. It is then that "man's extremity is God's opportunity." When man is at his wit's end, he is then in a position where the God-power can do the "impossible," because that is the nature of God, the Doer of the impossible. But many people arrive at their extremity and still hold on or die, "kicking against the pricks," fighting the appearances which they think are real and true.

When a situation in the human picture is immovable or a condition impregnable, there is a way of entering into this secret conspiracy with Jesus to come through it all, and that too without the smell of fire on your garments. It is not going to be a fight. Though you may pass through what seems a confusion of things, "yet shall it not come nigh thee"; yea, even though "ten thousand fall at thy right hand and left."

You are beginning to see that the ways of God are past finding out. The manner and means through which this new Light is to come to earth is not in the understanding of man but is in the care of God. And it is wonderful—praise God. Nothing is impossible to God. He has the way ye know not of, but it is the way of salvation.

Ways and means of manifestation are entirely out of our hands. We are not concerned how the signs will come into manifestation, only with the fact that they will; and in the most unexpected way since it is perpetually the unexpected that happens. Stop looking for a sign. Stop looking for a fulfillment, for all of these things are already done and completed in God and are only awaiting your recognition to come forth into manifestation.

Time after time, Jesus directs the mind back to the contemplation of God. Why? Because until we know something of God, we cannot possibly take off at the level that "all things are possible to God"— that is, to you. All things that you can find possible to God are possible to you. It seems to expand as you go into it, but in reality it is the changeless Presence, which is always the same and which is instantly available to you wherever you are and in whatever condition.

The "prayer and fasting" necessary to overcome these "impossible" things with which we are confronted is the pure, unrelenting recognition of God here, there, and everywhere, no matter where you are or in what condition. Do you hear and see what this love of God in your heart can and will mean to you? Prayer and fasting from the temptation to give in to the appearances that are about you and a steady looking right into the face of God, while you die to the old condition you have been in—the impossible condition. "No man shall see my face and live." No man can continue to live in his present condition and look into the face of this pure recognition of the presence of God.

Prayer and fasting, to many people, is an actual knee service with an empty stomach. How could this possibly interest the God of love? Many people believe that prayer and fasting means the deletion of every single joy of life and a crouching at the feet of a tyrant God for such a time as He sees fit to watch the rather pitiful performance. Even a tyrant of ancient or modern history would eventually tire of such horseplay. "Know ye not that ye are gods," made in the image and likeness of God?

Why will you say, "If you *possibly* can," to this magnificent Power? Don't you yet recognize that it *can* take place because it *has already* taken place in the Life of your Perfect Identity?

Parallel with this lovely Divine Destiny, you are traveling along in the muck of human fate, which you have brought upon yourself by tasting of the fruit of the Garden of Eden, whereby you decided that you too could be a creator and vie with God. All you have created is a hypnosis of evil, and this has continued to function in the place of evil ever since. When you awake to this beautiful truth, you will ascend to the Father-Consciousness, or the Permanent Identity, and instantly appropriate the status of Destiny there functioning. The world says you have had a perfect demonstration or an instantaneous demonstration, but you have merely blended yourself with the finished thing. Jesus always said, "It is done" — is consummated, completed.

Standing steadfast in this recognition is the "praying without ceasing." Everything you recognize of beauty and goodness in the world is prayer. You pray to a tree when you recognize its beauty, and you pray to a flower when you stand enraptured with its loveliness. And sometimes — dare I say this to you — you may get an acknowledgment of your prayer from a tree or a flower! Such things have happened. "I have many things to tell you," but most of them you will get between the lines because

115

they are not for the profane demonstrators of Truth. They are for the revelation of the higher Power which has become natural and real to you.

So watch, watch, watch; ye know not at what hour *I* come. I said you know not at what hour, so that makes it possible to happen almost anywhere—except where you go especially thinking it will happen or trying to make it happen by joining masses of emotional people who are proclaiming God as present.

"Believest thou that I am able to do this unto you?" Answer me. Do you—you, the reader, and for yourself alone—do you believe? Do you? Is the mist thinning and the "if you possibly can" melting out in the glorious revelation of "my Lord and my God?" Do you begin to understand a little?

In the illustration given, you are the father with the lunatic son. The lunatic son is your human personality that is so bound by limitations—sickness, sin, heredity, and environment—yea, and a hornet's nest of mistakes you have made, with their accompanying stings. You have been to every doctor, healer, teacher, leader, organization, and book, and still nothing has happened except that the wall of "if you *possibly* can" is more dense than ever.

And at last you have come to the Jesus Christ situation. Yes, you are right up to the place where you can ask the Power to heal your son; but you still interpose the "if you *possibly* can." And then that wonderful question that you must answer: "Why do you say *possibly*?"

One moment of this situation will melt all the rubbish and debris from your life, for you know that when you are born again, you are *born* again; and just as in reincarnation, when you are born again you are new—no matter what great wig or tyrant or leper you formerly were. You can take only a faint memory of it with you—and sometimes not that. So it says that "the former things are passed away; they shall not be remembered (by you or others), neither shall they come into mind any more (not any more)."

Do you begin to see that we are not telling you of a power that is man-made and limited to the findings of his foolish wisdom, but of the power of God, which is "quick and terrible and sharper than a two-edged sword, turning in all directions"? Can you imagine a two-edged sword whirling in all directions? Like to put your head in the way of it? Why not? When you put the head of your old human problem in the way of it, something is going to happen. It is all so wonderful and so simple that it is amazing.

There is something wonderful in this entering into a secret conspiracy with Jesus Christ. It is filled with inspiration that no man will ever tell you and that you cannot read in books—and yet you will know. You are in league with Light. All argument is gone. You begin to *know* God.

And so we hear the Father speaking to the deaf and dumb and blind spirits of human beliefs: "Come out of him and enter him no more." We hear the word of the Father cleansing the temple of the whole lot of evil spirits. They enter into the swinish manifestation of the human mind as a last effort to preserve themselves, but the madness of it rushes them over the cliffs into the sea of oblivion.

Once I heard a very refined and elegant woman who was very concerned about the poor swineherd and his pigs. She didn't see beyond the story, and it never occurred to her that at the very moment his swine were taken away from him, he may have been able to enter into the new dimension of Life.

While this is just parable, it all has a meaning for you. We are everything in the realm of the human, capable of doing everything evil as well as good, and we see in the Bible a thousand and one illustrations of the mind, human and divine. We orientate ourselves in order to get the most light on the present condition.

Sooner or later, everybody who is to enter in must and will bring his maniac son to the Father and have cast out of him the blindness and deafness and dumbness to the revelation of Jesus Christ.

The picture darkens as we see another maniacal condition of human thought. This time it is living in the graveyard, playing with dead men's bones. That might be a stack of old memories and love letters; they have caused thousands of people to live in the grave of the past. If you try to dislodge any of these memories and beliefs in past conditions, there is the crying out, "Go away; why have you come here to disturb us?" Why have you come here to clean out the temple of the past debris of our human life so that the light of God may shine through? It hurts the old human mind to let go because it would rather hang on to dead memories than enter into new and fresh situations of the new Life.

"And Jesus commanded," and "he fell as one dead." There was so little left by the time he got through with his memories and beliefs in the lies with which he had stored his house that he was empty for the moment. But wait a moment—the floods of Light in Jesus Christ are infixing him with the breath of Life, and he is healed, changed, born anew into the new day of God.

As you begin to understand the difference between the impossible and the possible in its true interpretation, you will be taken up to the level of consciousness where you will be allowed actually to see the dissemination of the hard, fast pictures of the human consciousness, and how it is that the love of God actually melts the frozen human thought and transforms it into Light. You will then be able to see the *real* nature of the belief which is affecting another, not just the results of that belief. And by "opening your mouth" and letting the Word speak through you, you will bring the panacea or the manifestation into being.

Believest thou this? Or would you like it to be so? It can never be so in the human thought. You cannot bring God down to that level, for it is only a hypnotic level of thought and exists only to you.

Yes, you too will understand "the temple of the living God" and will know, actually, that every manifestation on the earth is the temple of the body of God and that any of them can function in any capacity necessary. *I* am always with you — remember this — and *I* need only to have a temple through which to express, whether it is yours or another's.

Remember the "burning bush," or do you? Or do you believe such stuff? You have never seen any of it and never will until you can believe in God, and then many things will take place quite naturally that formerly seemed like the works of a Tibetan Lama; and wonder of wonders, they will happen to you — this funny little old thing that has never had anything, done anything, or had any chances.

If you cannot go into a certain city (state of consciousness) which actually recognizes God as present, you naturally cannot find the man (temple) which is to show you the upper chamber, and so you cannot have the banquet, and so you will be hungry — and so and so and so ... Do you begin to see what I am saying to you about the secret conspiracy with Jesus Christ?

The maniac son wants to know, "How do you get into this consciousness?" And the answer from the reasoning human mind is as maddening as can be. It is simply, "Go." That makes the old mind that has wisdom that is "foolishness in the eyes of God" see red, and he wants to make something out of it— but it won't fit.

You cannot put Infinity into the pattern of finity, and so you cannot put Divine Wisdom into the limitation of human foolishness called thought.

Chapter XI

Soul and Living Soul

*And he breathed into him the breath of life,
and he became a living soul.*

Ever think about it? No? Well.

There must be some difference between soul and Living Soul, and that difference is just this: until you become conscious of the Permanent Identity within you—the Father within you, the real you— you are merely a soul, moving about in a body, or temple, and that soul apparently subject to every law of matter—birth, growth, maturity, and decay— and its life measured by the three-dimensional laws of matter. "As for man, his days are few and full of trouble." There is no escape from the hateful human destiny, and the soul must plod along through the muddy vestures of life as best he can until he can reach the grave.

But suddenly he discovers he is inbreathed with the breath of Life, and he becomes a Living Soul; the dead thing becomes alive; the consciousness of his Permanent Identity reverses the order of life and takes over the control, and he discovers that he is born of God. "Call no man your father" takes place when man becomes a Living Soul—when he suddenly realizes for the first time that he is inbreathed with the breath of Life and that he has become alive, alive to a world which "eyes have not seen and ears have not heard." He becomes conscious of many things which have never before entered his ken but which are already prepared. Isn't it wonderful that they are already prepared — he doesn't have to prepare them; he has only to appropriate and use and make them his own.

The job you took on when you came here was called by your name. After a short while, the John Smith you had taken over became well known to you — his faults and weaknesses and his good points — but you were sure you could get hold of that manifestation and transform it and cause it to be a real temple of God. But somehow or other, through it all, the thought-pictures of human things became too real, and perhaps you got so thoroughly lost in the John Smith destiny that you finally became hopelessly involved and asked yourself, "What am I here for anyway?" and many more questions of like nature. But occasionally some John Smith has realized his Permanent Identity and has been able to experience the thrilling sense of being inbreathed with the breath of God and becoming a Living Soul. And so right there, in the midst of the confusion of the John Smith pattern, has begun the transformation, the change from corruptible to incorruptible.

Sometimes, when the soul could do nothing with its John Smith, it just kicked it off through disease or accident—got rid of it, so to speak, because it could do nothing with it. But in this day and age, the New Power is descending upon the earth, and thousands who are now dead shall be made alive; thousands who are lost in the congestion of John Smith consciousness shall be inbreathed and be made Living Souls. They shall suddenly *see* the Light through the recognition of the simple teaching of Jesus Christ. "Be still, and know that I am God."

In the hush of being newly born, in the hush of the New Day, you retire to the stable of your heart and there experience the "inbreathing" of the Lord. You become a Living Soul, and the coal of fire goes on your lips. The precious thing has happened to you. It may yet have a long way to come before it will be glorified, but already the light is penetrating. The leaven is leavening the whole mass of meal. You are being born again and being made new, and this time it is the precious secret and sacred doctrine.

No more babbling to the man in the street. When the time comes for you to speak, you will speak the Word, and it shall be productive of results. And the curious, the filthy, who are peeping to see a miracle, shall remain filthy still. They shall see nothing; they shall have nothing given to them but the long, hot walk back from the desert where they went to "seek me after loaves and fishes." What do you care whether they believe or not? If they cannot see God, it is because they have no love of God in their hearts; they have been seeking Him after *things,* and there are no more things left because every thing is left behind.

"Ye seek me, but ye cannot find me." Watch— even the very elect may be led astray; so follow no man, woman, book, organization. "Follow me." Do you hear!

So you become a Living Soul. You leave the tomb of John Smith, and there comes the wonderful word of protection, "Touch me not," to all those who would like to handle with their hands and examine what they call miracles.

> Be still. Be very still
> And deeply quiet.
> You are a Living Soul.
> It is well with thee.

Chapter XII

There Is No Shortage in God

There is no shortage in God. The only shortage is in the human thought. The Infinite contains all. Nothing is lost; nothing is taken from the All. Nothing is added. It is One Indivisible, unchangeable.

This ceases to be a dogmatic statement of God or a definition of Jehovah when you see the practical demonstration of this truth by the Elder Brother Jesus.

There was a shortage of bread and fish in the minds of five thousand men, and that shortage in their minds was deduced from what they saw, heard, and felt in the relative world. But in the mind of God there was no shortage, so the moment Jesus ascended to his own Fatherhood degree, He was able to contact this fact and bring it down into the congested human thought of man, in the form of substance.

The moment He brought forth the bread and fish, there was no shortage in the mind of man, for the moment at least. "He will keep him in perfect peace, whose mind is stayed" on Him. He whose mind is stayed on the consciousness of God remains in perfect peace, for while he does not carry a load of material provisions or substance around with him, he has the instant ability to enter into the Fatherhood degree and reveal what the human mind cannot see because of the congestion of human thought.

Human thought becomes congested because it judges from appearances instead of "judging righteous judgment." Jesus (John Smith, you) ascending into the Fatherhood degree reveals the Christ (Permanent Identity, the real You). Jesus does not create. A miracle is not something that adds to or takes from; it reveals the true state of Life and displaces the congested thought-pictures that have formed on the body, the temple of God.

There is no absence of God in the universe, and there is no shortage of anything in God. But the human thought cannot *see* God. The human thought "dies" the moment it sees God ("No man shall see my face and live")—dies to the present state of thought-congestion and enters into a new level of revelation.

We are here for the purpose of revealing that which *is*, not for curing or destroying anything. "I came not to destroy, but to fulfill," and so the "coming" of the Father into expression is merely the revelation of that which eternally *is*. The congested human thought-picture is broken up, as it were, and the new form appears. Just as steel—although long ago hardened into thousands of different shapes—may all be put back into the melting pot and poured into entirely new molds, so the congested or evil-shaped pictures of matter are not permanently hard, fast shapes and forms, and the moment the Life substance is seen for what it is, the fashion of it is changed. "The fashion of his countenance was changed." All this wonderful idea will develop in you as you quietly learn to pray the prayer, "Be still, and know that I am God," and see that there is nothing lacking (no matter what the senses say) in God.

In Him you live and breathe and move and have your being; and inversely, He lives and breathes and moves and has His being in you. Stop for a moment and contemplate that state of affairs, and you will see something you have not been able to see before. A New Day is dawning, and you are entering in and are being saved from the congested thought-pictures of the world, which is rapidly passing away.

Yes, the world of human congested thought-pictures shall pass away, but "My word shall not pass away." Do you hear? Do you believe?

There was limitation and lack in the minds of the wedding guests. They formed their limited pictures through a series of events which were perfectly natural and real. Half a hundred guests had been wining and dining, and they had consumed all the wine. Well, that was a fact. They hadn't wasted it. There were just so many gallons of wine and so many men, and it actually, literally, had been consumed before their eyes. Wasn't the picture that followed quite natural—no wine?

Yes, and it was true, as all the pictures of human congested thought are true. So a diseased condition which has eaten away part of your body is true to the congested human thought—but it is not true to God, and it takes only the recognition of this Presence to reveal what the unmanifest Christ of you knows eternally as a reality.

So you begin to see that the day of miracle-making has come to an end. It had its purpose, and now comes the day of entering into the Fatherhood degree, where it is quite natural to set aside the congested pictures of human thinking. "I will go unto my Father ... I will ask my Father ... I and my Father are One ... ."

Yes, I think it is time you started to search the Scriptures. Not to find out some prophecy about the end of the world or to ascertain how soon your enemies are to be destroyed, but for Life eternal. "This is life eternal"—to know Me, the true, living substance of God here and now.

Do you begin to see? I am asking you something. Don't hurry over this. Do you begin to *see* a little? Perceive? Extend that vision into Reality!

A handful of meal, a few drops of oil, dregs of wine, five loaves and two fishes—that is what the picture shows. Well, there it is. Anyone can see it, handle it, speculate upon it, and come to the conclusion, by every scientific measurement, that there is no more and that by no possible flight of imagination can be made a barrel of oil from a few drops or five thousand loaves from five. That would be rank idiocy on the relative plane, and it could not take place. Nothing takes place on that plane but that you consume what you have, and that is the end of it all, whether it be health, money, happiness, etc. There is no argument. It is so. And remember, we are not trying to prove that it is not so, for it is so on that plane, and there is only one thing to do about it—go out and work by the sweat of your brow and get some more.

Anyone will tell you that and prove it to you. So if you are still trying to prove things by the Power, you are wasting your time. It doesn't have to be proved—it has to be revealed; and strangely enough, through you—you, the funny little thing which just a few moments ago was bemoaning the fact that you had but three drops of oil left between you and starvation. That isn't much joy, is it? Just three drops ... but ... well, what are you going to do about it?

> Do you believe in God, or man and what he has found out? Do you believe in the shortage, or in the abundance of God?

Chapter XIII

No Man Hath Revealed
This unto Thee

"No man hath revealed this unto thee" or me. That which is coming through into manifestation in these latter days is not the result of something revealed unto thee by man. It is the result of that which has been revealed to thee by the Father within. As soon as we begin to realize this, even in a small way, we begin also to have eyes that *see* what the Spirit saith unto the churches (temple-bodies) of mankind.

"Ask of the Lord," and hear the revelation within the temple of your own being, within the temple of the living God, within the "temple not made with hands, but eternal in the heavens." Yea, ask what ye will. Do you hear? And it *shall* (not maybe or perhaps) be revealed unto thee!

As flesh and blood in the matter-sense of life cannot inherit the kingdom of heaven because of the density of human thought, neither can this matter-flesh-and-blood reveal anything unto you. The only thing it can do is to show the results of the consciousness of the Father within, but it remains void of any power to be a first mover, as it were.

"Not that which goeth in, but that which cometh out makes or defiles a man." It is that which cometh out through the consciousness of you which makes or defiles. And that is why we are even now changing and transmuting matter into Spirit and Spirit into matter and are being able to *see God in the flesh*—this new-blended substance of which the temple of the living God is made; a temple so plastic and fluidic that it can mirror forth instantly the Word or the thing which has been told in secret. And so, "The Father, seeing in secret, shall reward thee openly."

"No man hath revealed this unto thee," and therefore it belongs to no man or organization. As long as a so-called truth belongs to a man or an organization, it is colored to such an extent by that person or group of persons that it is practically worthless. But "no man hath revealed this unto thee" is something different, for what it reveals becomes *your* personal revelation, which in turn is released to the world in which *you* live.

It is this wonderful sweep of Light which brings its infinite changes in a changeless Principle. It shows forth "the invisible things of Spirit." Just as the white light is found to have all the colors of the rainbow within it, so the Father-Consciousness within you is ready to reveal so much more than man has ever thought of or could ever accept or understand.

The literal interpretation of the name *Jesus* is "reality tends to liberate." Do you begin to see why the name (nature) of Jesus brings such freedom to the captive? But this is not revealed unto thee by man. It is the gift of Spirit which is within thee, waiting to be stirred up: the nature of Jesus Christ—Jesus (Reality tends to liberate) and the power of the Christ to carry it through into releasement into the kingdom of heaven. It is wonderful. And as you serenely contemplate this revelation of Jesus Christ, you will enter into your inheritance and be at peace. New and awe-inspiring things will gradually become visible as this new day of self-revelation takes place in you.

Yes, "I saw thee under the fig tree" is part of the holy revelation that is coming through to you. You, also, will be able to see what is "under the fig tree" and to understand just what is being presented to you at all times, no matter what its covering; and this will give you the power to walk over the waves of human limitations. You will launch out into deeper waters and find the sailing more harmonious, for you are leaving the shallows of human reasoning for the deeps of the Christ-wisdom.

You begin to feel a fearlessness of the journey, an assurance you have not yet known, and to understand why it is no longer necessary to "take thought" of this journey through life. You are receiving the revelation which does not have to be slowed down to the tedious thought-taking processes of mankind. In the twinkling of an eye, all is changed before your very eyes, for "flesh and blood have not revealed it unto thee," but the Spirit of the Lord has come unto you and given you a new name.

Singing in the heart of you is this glorious truth: "No man hath revealed this unto thee." No man could. Your recognized Christ hath revealed it to you; and as you press farther into this Light, you will begin to *see* and to *know* something of the height and depth and majesty of the Lord in which you live, move, breathe, and have your being. *You* have your being, or actual existence, in this God, and so the moment you enter into this Presence consciously, you begin to *live*, to experience Life.

No man hath revealed
this unto thee. Do you hear?

Chapter XIV

Assumption

He made himself as God.

What are you going to do about it—crucify him again? Remembering that you crucified Him once before for doing the same thing, what will you do with the second coming of the principle of Christ Jesus? Unless He had made himself as God, He could not have done the works of God but would have remained a carpenter.

"He made himself as God." Can you stand it? Or in modern language, "Can you take it?" Do you believe, in the first place, that it is possible? Is there any of that hypocritical belief left in you that wants to find out about it all before it believes? Are you looking for the Truth, or some *system* of Truth invented in the nineteenth century? Do you want the Truth for the love of the Truth, or do you want It for what you can get out of It?

Suppose we took away all the glory and the pay of "the work." Would you still be interested, or do you want a big church, a radio, a board of directors, all to carry forth the lovely work of the one who said, "Consider the lilies"—not on the latest millinery creation but in the glorious open fields of God! What are you after? Things? Demonstrations?

Or are you after the revelation of Life, which includes all things, even the new hat you want or the luxury car, strange as it may seem. But can you take it? You have heard this before, in the more beautiful poetic language: "Believest thou this?"

It is glorious when we bring our Jesus right down to today and see that He was a man who discovered the principle of Life and had a burning desire to share it with the world—but "ye would not." You had to get your little human intelligence in the way and see whether it was going to recognize *you* as something.

You profess to believe in God, to follow Jesus Christ, the Wayshower. Or do you? What do you want with Me? A part of My robe, or all of it? Do you want the loaves and the fishes, or the Substance out of which they came? Did you see the miracle and seek Me because of that, or do you just want some bread and fish?

Well, we have a little concentration to do; we have a moment when perhaps it is best to "enter into the closet and shut the door." What do you say? What seek ye? The living among the dead? What are you after? You—yes, you, the reader. Ask yourself. What *are* you after? Do you want Truth and Life, or do you want a new hat or a car? Answer me!

Does it make you rather ashamed to be present in a group of people, assembled in a temple of God, asking for new hats and cars? Does it seem rather unholy and terrible, in spite of the lordly voice advising that God will supply your every need? Don't you feel ashamed? Or do you? In this glorious revelation, the All is given to you whenever you are ready to accept It, as a natural thing instead of a demonstration.

Presently you will understand how it is that "things" are merely the solidification of the "substance of things hoped for" which is all about you; and you will also see that ice can be melted into water, heated into steam, and put under such a terrific heat that it becomes invisible right before your very eyes. A piece of ice cast on a hot stove disappears as you watch, a clear example of the power to "pick it up or lay it down."

When you "leave all and follow me," you leave nothing but the burden of human responsibility. When you see that "things" are merely the shadow cast from the matrix of consciousness, then you will understand how it is that you can use and enjoy the things without the worry that they are going away from you. As long as you have a thing in consciousness, you will be able to reproduce it over and over again.

Visualization will get you nowhere but into a bog of human thought, for visualization is merely the hypnosis of human thought. A person visualizing himself as handling thousands of dollars might find himself a clerk in a bank at fifteen dollars a week. He could handle all sorts of money, perhaps millions of dollars, but it would not be his. And so with all the foolishness of visualization.

Consciousness is an entirely different thing. It is back of all manifestation, and it comes most easily through the assumption of your God-heritage. "He made himself as God" then comes as a revelation, not as a miracle or a freak of some strange power. The moment you make yourself one with any state of consciousness, you manifest easily and naturally all that that consciousness has to give forth, instead of having to make a demonstration of a nineteenth century idea of God.

Remember, God existed in all His fullness long before any of the present-day organizations, advertised as having discovered God, were ever conceived. From the ads, one would imagine that a South African hunter had discovered the skeleton of a mammal on which he was constructing a body of flesh. But God has always been here and will always be here, regardless of organization, book, teacher, or preacher. And He is unchangeable. Do you hear? Unchangeable, quite regardless of politics and customs.

It must be natural, normal, and easy if we are to get into this "kingdom of heaven." It is given to the child, and no amount of intellectual reasoning or work will bring it to pass. All this seems stupid to the human intellect that is so wise in its own conceit; but it is *wisdom* we are after, not the intelligence of the three-dimensional mind.

Strange how we should still be fighting against this lovely gift; but are you ready to let go of the human personality, as Jesus did when He went unto his Father, remembering that, "all things will be added"? When you seek the kingdom of heaven, you are entering into the Oneness, and the things necessary will be added, remembering also that the signs shall follow—they do not precede.

Isn't it glorious? You are coming out from among them. You have dehypnotized yourself from the "crowd" thing. There is little or no truth where crowds gather. So many are looking for bread and fishes that they blur out the very revelation of Jesus Christ and put up their idol, which sooner or later will be brought low because of its clay feet. Sooner or later, all the organizations that are in the business of "selling" God, no matter however holy they may appear, will be found to have clay feet and will go into the dust.

What seek ye? You, the reader—what do you want? Can you recognize the Truth alone, or is a crowd of people a sign that the Truth has come to earth? It is time that you were awake. When you understand what the Truth is, you will know that constant and stereotyped repetition causes It to lose all Its flavor. Inspiration is destroyed when Truth becomes a habit. Even the habit of "praying" at a set time and going over a set of rules eventually turns to dust. Going to the same place day after day and listening to the words of so-called inspired speakers finally causes a revulsion of feeling.

Do you begin to see that the inspiration is not trapped into man-made forms? It can come anytime and anywhere, the moment you recognize the Presence, even in hell. It is not necessarily found in so-called holy places. "Take off your shoes; this is holy ground," could be said to you no matter where you were standing.

If you have to have a certain pew or choir or leader to give you the truth, you might some time get caught miles from the old home base. You might! A bee can extract honey from a poisonous flower. Can you? Why not? Suppose you were starving and had to. What then? "My sheep hear my voice." And so it is.

In the assumption to which we refer, we find an actual appropriation of Consciousness. "He made himself as God." Not God, but *as* God—of the same nature and substance. He discovered that, "made in the image and likeness of God," He was actually that which He assumed Himself to be. Hence, He could "speak as one having authority," and hence, He had the ability to "go thou and do likewise."

When the human mind assumes anything, it is merely bluffing, trying to make something happen or trying to make someone believe he is something that he is not. No matter how clever the assumption is, sooner or later comes a cleverer mind than his and overturns him. There is always a chink in the armor through which the rapier-like human mind can pass with its killing sting.

Whitewashing the outside of an old building does not make it new. If it is rotten, the only thing that will help it is to put up a new structure. And so whitewashing the old human thought-structure and trying to make it look like something it is not is a waste of time. Presently it will cave in and fall. And likewise, you either *hear*, or you merely listen and hear nothing, for when you *hear*, you find yourself able to do or to have or to go, and so on.

There is a divine indifference to the "former things" and beliefs, and this divine indifference is, in reality, understanding of the higher laws of Life and indifference to the former beliefs. All this is hidden in secrecy, in a place of inner solitude, a retreat where actual silence exists; and in this place you *hear* the still small voice and are instructed about the journey you are to make.

All this is written to you in the joy of revelation. You must make your assumption, which is divinely possible to you because Jesus gave it to you when He commanded, "The works that I do, ye shall do also, and even greater works than these," outlining for you step by step the progress you were to make, easily and naturally, and then even indicating works you were to do which transcended the works already done—"greater works shall ye do." No maybe or perhaps. Greater works *shall* you do when

141

you "make yourself as God" and move out into that level of consciousness.

"Go in and possess the land." How can you, unless you make your assumption of ownership? Unless you actually own the land, you cannot go in and possess it, for you will be thrown out for trying to take something that does not belong to you. Do you understand that things which are yours on the fourth-dimensional plane are not yours on the third? For instance, you cannot have absolute health on the three-dimensional plane of life, for it does not exist there and is not true, and so with wealth, happiness, etc.

Since you have already done everything possible to help yourself and have failed to bring out the sense of Life which you have desired, it is time you entered into the consciousness of Jesus Christ and discovered the power which lies there, ready and waiting to be utilized. "I can do all things through Christ Jesus," remembering that Jesus was a man, that Christ is a principle, and that Jesus Christ is the state of consciousness where matter is spiritualized and where Spirit is materialized. It is the place of transition, or the stepping-up point. The invisible becomes visible, and the visible becomes invisible when passed through this Consciousness.

All this is rather crudely put in our three-dimensional language, and it is necessary to gather from between the lines the real import of this revelation. "Yet in my (my own) flesh shall I see

God." As has been explained before, flesh, in this sense of the word, is the result of blending Spirit and matter.

Well, Mary "pondered these things in her heart." What will you do with them? They are contrary to everything that the human mind knows and believes. It is impossible to prove them, and yet that is exactly what you must do. It all seems to be full of paradoxes; but only to the human thinking, which has no proper basis to stand upon, for it doesn't really know where it came from or how. Its foundation is quite as fantastic as accounts of creation in pagan religions. It is finally up against a wall. From the chicken, the egg; from the egg, the chicken—where did it all begin?

It began at the moment man took upon himself the business of being a creator in a world or heaven which was already completely created, and hence, he has created but the inventions of his own limitations. Man has worked out "many inventions." You have worked out a good many in your own life pattern. None of them has any more foundation than the inventions of other minds. Their foundation is "a liar and the father of it," so why will you hesitate to "leave all and follow me"?

You can convince no one else by talk or argument, and that is why the "coal of fire" must be placed on your lips. "See that ye tell no man—show John." Keep silent before Me, and let the earth (the manifestation you have brought out) renew itself.

A complete rejuvenation is taking place; everything is being made new, and you have entered into this inner solitude, a place where nothing enters, where nothing matters, where you are at the listening-post of Life to "hear what the Spirit has to say."

"To him that overcometh" shall I give the keys to the kingdom. This overcoming is not a battle. It is actually the assumption of your God-heritage, the entering into your Christ-Consciousness; and it is this overcoming which gives you the keys, the understanding, to undo or unlock all the combinations of human thinking.

All your desires and wishes, when properly interpreted, are good and should be fulfilled: "I shall give you the desires of your heart" indicates that the desires in your heart will be fulfilled when rightly interpreted.

A bank robber desires money. There is nothing wrong in that; so has the most saintly desired the wherewithal to purchase the needed things in life. What is wrong is the robber's interpretation of how to get it. He looks out on a world of inequalities and sees all the money tied up in one place. His desire seeks one way after another to get his "substance," and finally it enters into the evil of the human mind and tries to force it away from its owner. A man who kills another more than likely has only one idea in mind—he wishes to rid himself of something evil that is keeping from him his harmony. But his interpretation is wrong.

So with you. The desire you have is of God, but its interpretation is all wrong. Through the "glass darkly" of human thinking and false education, you have come to a manifestation as distorted and twisted as can be. Your desire for health manifests itself through all the false education of sickness and disease. You try a thousand and one ways to fulfill your desire, and you, like the bank robber, are thrown into prison.

When Mary had the annunciation of what was to take place, she was as helpless with the idea as you would be. A million questions no doubt flooded her mind. How? Why? When? Where? She could no more work out this annunciation or desire than you could. Surely, if she had wanted to name it a problem, its answer would have been greater than anything with which you have been confronted. But Mary pondered these things in her heart and made the assumption that God was able to do things that man could not even think of, and so the Messiah was put on earth. The idea or desire took on a body and form and was sent into manifestation "by the way ye know not of" and in a manner which none could anticipate. So will it be with you and your desire when you are willing and ready to *let* the power into operation.

All this lovely mystical affair can take place only in the heart that has long since ceased to believe in the foolishness of man's wisdom and has come to an actual *belief* in God. All the attempts to prove this law, curiosity to see whether or not it will work, have been wasted. There can be no curiosity in the mind that has made its assumption, for you have come to the place of pure and absolute recognition that it is so. And trying to see or attempting to make something happen only indicates that you have not yet arrived at the place of "belief in God." When you have arrived you will know—and the signs will follow.

Assuming that your desires are already fulfilled ("Before you ask, I will answer"), you are then freed from the tedious work of *trying* to assist the birth of the new manifestation. You stand at attention, willing and ready to lend yourself and body in any way to carry out the ideas presented by the inner urge, but at the same time you keep entirely out of the way. "Let the child be born" does not mean *make* the child be born. There is a vast difference.

As has been explained, your desires are really the things in their incipiency pressing upon you for expression, and so the whole process is reversed. We do not get a desire and have to work it out or cause it to take place. The reason we have a desire is because the thing is ready to take place—the child is crying out in the invisible for a body. "The ways of God are past understanding."

"Thus he (the character referred to) daily prepared himself, all unconscious that he was so

146

doing, for the magical Presence which is about us everywhere—not quite out of sight, not quite out of hearing, but too often lost, unheard, and unseen in the tumult of the world and the engulfing onrush of egoism. That old eternal Presence which listens to no argument, reveals Itself to no strangers, he was rediscovering daily by himself in the poetry and prose of mere circumstance."

Gradually, the old human doubting mind will give way before the presence of this assumption. There will be hours, yea, sometimes days, of meditation and contemplation; hours filled with the unspeakable vision; hours wherein you will see All and know the answers before the questions; hours wherein will be revealed to you secret doctrines never yet written or spoken.

Chapter XV

Then Abraham Laughed

And the Lord said of Sarah: And I will bless her, and give thee a son of her; yea, I will bless her, and she shall be a mother of nations; kings of people shall be of her.

Then Abraham fell upon his face, and laughed, and said in his heart, Shall a child be born unto him that is an hundred years old? And shall Sarah, that is ninety years old, bear?"

No wonder Abraham laughed when he thought of such an impossible thing as bearing a child at ninety. It had never happened before, and it was utterly impossible so far as he knew; but the Lord said that Sarah would bring forth a child at ninety.

What are you going to do about it? Deny it? Argue about it? Try to twist it around to suit your own notion? Or are you beginning to believe that the Spirit you have spoken of so long is the doer of the impossible and the *only* doer of the impossible? Everything that is impossible to the human mind is possible to God. What have you to say about that? Believe it? Or deny it?

"Yes I know, but ... "and, "Be reasonable." If you are "reasonable," you are using human limitations, and your present problem is just as impossible of being solved as Sarah bringing forth a child at ninety; yet the Lord said, "She shall bring forth a child" at ninety.

These marvelous citations are given in order that you may glimpse the power of Almighty God in contradistinction to the thought-forces which you have used for so long and which have failed to accomplish "whereunto they were sent."

"What? You mean to heal this incurable disease? It is impossible, for this is a condition that has never been touched by anything. Don't make me laugh with your absurd promises that I can be well," (that I can suddenly perceive the difference between the ways of God and the ways of man and learn that the ways of God "are past finding out" and are in no way concerned with the concrete belief of human thought).

The ways of God are past finding out. The ways and means of bringing the impossible into visibility, of offsetting and overturning the best established beliefs of man and organizations are past the speculation of human thought. No sooner are you confronted with a problem in your life than you measure it by relative findings and pronounce it incurable. At that moment you contact all the race-consciousness of that particular problem, and it is intensified a thousandfold.

If you have heart trouble and have accepted it as such, you are at once in league with the sum total of the world-consciousness on that subject. The next move is to verify its findings, and so you see your heart trouble written in letters of fire against a black sky. You find it everywhere, because there is agreement with evil all over the world. Everything you contact gives added proof of that which you have accepted as true.

Having once accepted it as true, you then begin fighting it vigorously. You deny it. You affirm something that is supposed to heal it. You fight it with material weapons. And at every move, you find it more and more aggravated and intense. Everything seems leagued in a subtle conspiracy to prove true what you have accepted as true. That is in accordance with the law, for the pattern you hold in consciousness must be made manifest.

Working from the mental basis when trying to overcome this belief only intensifies it. You are faced with the idea of a new birth ("Ye must be born again"), and while this sounds as terrific and impossible to you as it did to Nicodemus, once you perceive that it is to be accomplished, not by the way of man but by the way of God, you instantly open a door of escape.

No wonder Abraham laughed when he heard such a fairy tale about Sarah. So do you laugh, in your human state of consciousness, when you hear that from your present prison of belief, age, disease, or what you will, you have a perfect means of escape into the fulfillment of your desire. You are so hypnotized with the findings of the world that you are skeptically amused that anyone would say it was possible for you to bring forth your desire.

But know that the moment you arrive at any spiritual state, you have always been there. In reality, that is so.

> Never for one moment has your Permanent Identity stopped functioning on the spiritual plane; and though you have drifted for years, or even centuries, in the uncharted waters of human thinking, your ark suddenly comes to haven on Mount Ararat, salvaged by the revelation of Jesus Christ.
>
> The moment you accomplish anything in the way of the higher Consciousness, former things and beliefs pass away, and even the memory of it "is no more." So you cannot even recall the time when you were under the curse of the law of disease or poverty. From the moment you touch the consciousness of health and prosperity in the mind of God, you have always been in the place of health and plenty.

It is wonderful how the light is suddenly coming to you. Every move in the revelation of Light is a gain. You cannot revert to the former state. "The former things have passed away."

Suppose you are faced with a condition that is quite as humanly impossible as the bringing forth of a child at ninety. Are you going to break out into ribald laughter? Will the sudden revelation of the possibility of this thing which cannot happen to you be "laughed to scorn," as was the Master, Jesus, when he said something above the scope of the human intellect? Are you ready to hear the Word and obey the Voice and find *all* the wisdom of man "foolishness in the eyes of God?" Or are you making some reservations, such as, "Yes, I know, but this is different; my case … " etc., etc. Answer me!

Do you *believe,* or do you believe? Do you believe the word of God, or are you dividing it? The "house divided against itself shall fall," and so the consciousness that believes only partly in God and more wholly in evil shall drop to the level of its most human thought.

So you have to have a child at ninety? You have to find a job when there is none? You have to cure an incurable disease? You have to find happiness in a world of woe? And when you are told to go ahead and have the child at ninety, then you laugh the incredulous laugh of the mental consciousness, which says, "Well, go ahead and try it, but let me see the sign."

"Thou fool! Do you not know that a seed must first fall into the ground and rot before it can be made alive?" Do you suppose the consciousness that laughed, the consciousness ninety years old, could have conceived that new idea? Do you think for a moment that you are going to graft this new revelation onto the old, worn-out consciousness with which you have been working lo these many years?

This old consciousness knows it is all so ridiculous, that it is "nothing but talk," a narcotic to put you to sleep; and so it is, from the relative standpoint, because the wisdom of God is foolishness in the eyes of man. The ways of God are neither understandable nor possible to man, so he discounts the whole thing as something worse than absurd.

"Awake thou that sleepest." This new revelation can no more take place with you in your present state of consciousness than it could with Abraham while he was skeptical in regard to Sarah. The marvelous thing is that when the urge comes or the Voice and Word send forth a decree, the ways and means of its taking place are with it. For wrapped up in every desire is the means of expressing itself.

Do you hear? You do not get the power from without or from some affirmation. The desire has within itself this seed of power which, when once recognized, begins its expansion until it has broken the shell or pattern of its present limitation and the new order has set in. The incurable disease and the fear that you have about it will both be shattered by the Power which is wrapped up in the desire for health you have within you, which Power only awaits your calling it by name (Jesus Christ).

Is your condition comparable with bearing a child at ninety? The medical world would charge the latter off to religious hallucination, and your own people will charge off your possible healing to imagination. They believe it is just as out of the question as did Abraham when he heard that Sarah was to bear a child.

It is interesting that Abraham laughed because he did not think it possible (and any reasoning person would agree). Neither does anyone believe that you can bring out what you are seeking to produce. Yet when once you hear the Voice saying, "You shall bring forth a child at ninety," know that the ways and means will be provided and that it will all be natural.

The only thing that is not natural about the situation of bringing forth a child at ninety is your belief and acceptance of age. That is something that has to do with thought and not with man made in the image of God. It is something that man has conceived as a measure of Life. Yet Life is without beginning or end and has no age. God is no older now than He was at the beginning. The only age existent is the record of events in your life.

"God hath made me to laugh, so that all that hear will laugh with me." Thus saith Sarah. She has the proof of this wonderful urge of Spirit to do the impossible, and do you note that she is laughing? Her laugh is joyous recognition. "I have gotten a man from the Lord."

So will you suddenly burst out in joyous laughter, and this laughter will shatter old beliefs of death and so flood your temple with light and joy that all the parts of it shall be again fresh and new, and the light shall search the joints and marrow.

"And Sarah said, God hath made me to laugh so that all that hear will laugh with me." Again, it does not say "all." It says, "all that hear," for there are many that will not hear the laughter of God and will not be able to attain the planes of light and revelation which make the divine event possible. They cannot discover the place thereof because they cannot hear the laughter of Sarah. They are so busy laughing with Abraham that they have missed the whole event.

Take heed, lest it so be with you. Rather, be you so engrossed in recognizing the Power and magnifying the Lord within you that *your* child (heart's desire) may be born. The ways and means will take care of themselves, and before you know it, the laughter of God will burst over you, and you will cause many who hear to rejoice and to give thanks that "the Lord Omnipotent reigneth." It is wonderful.

Sarah laughed. Why? Because she was inspired to gala laughter by the sudden revelation that the thing which was utterly impossible was actually happening. Yes, in spite of every man-made law, it was coming to pass. The joke was on the human law.

You too will burst forth into laughter — at first, deep within your Soul, a silent, glorious light-laughter, which, as it nears the surface of your temple, will break out into a joyous, audible thanksgiving as the Word is made flesh within you and through you, and you launch forth your manifestation, knowing that your Redeemer liveth.

No matter what your problem is or how longstanding or how hateful and ugly it may appear, it is nothing to be compared with the allotment given Sarah. The child had to be born when it could not be formed. It had to come forth when everyone was laughing at the idea, even her husband; and yet this came to pass. Why? Because it was conceived as possible in the heart, not in the head. The difference is great and wonderful, for in the heart does one feel or sense realities, and in the head does one reduce the same to utter impossibilities. Thought is the killer that destroys everything which does not fit or conform to its false education.

Sarah is sometimes interpreted to mean "bitter," and we see how, out of this bitter-to-the-taste, hopeless state of affairs, something glorious took place that seemingly could not take place. You will see how everything in the parable indicates that the thing which you are attempting to bring forth is as nothing to that which has already been done. And this very revelation causes you to burst forth in laughter. And this very joyous laughter of recognition breaks away the hard and fast beliefs that have formed about your desire. It is released and set free, and its name is also called Isaac (sometimes interpreted *Laughter*)—Child of Promise.

At ninety you shall bring forth a child! Isn't it wonderful? A serenity settles in upon you as you begin actually to believe in God and in Me who was sent by God.

> Unlatch the sandals; you are standing on holy ground. You are in the presence of the power of God made manifest. And you shall bring forth a child at ninety. Laugh then. Shout for joy! The Lord Omnipotent reigneth!

Chapter XVI

It Is Done

Follow me.

At this stage of your ongoing, it is all or nothing. Either you are going to follow Me or you are still carrying in your pack or "burden" some man-made ideas, beliefs, or organizations. You are told to cast your burdens on Me, the burden of accumulated beliefs which have crystallized and become hard and fast shells that bind you. The history of your case, the history of your race, creed, etc., all the mistakes you have made and regretted, and above all, all your desires that have been unfulfilled—these are your burden.

So in your present shell you are bound. That shell is not capable of expressing the dreams of your soul. It has not the capacity or the ability to do so. These vile bodies, shapes, patterns must be changed, if that glorious Power or idea is to be expressed in you. If you could express your desires in your present consciousness or pattern, you would have done so long ago. But a reckoning shows that you have spent years trying to make them happen.

You could not literally give your desires a body, because you are "barren." There is not the inherent capacity in your present consciousness to accomplish the necessary steps to allow the new idea to come into manifestation. As a million volts of electricity cannot pass through a ten-volt wire, so the "greater things than these shall ye do" cannot function in a consciousness which is set fast in the belief that these things are impossible.

"Follow me." We have at least arrived at one point of understanding, which is that Jesus, the body-temple, did find a way out of the hard-fast patterns and beliefs that bound Him.

"Follow me." You begin to follow this design set by Jesus Christ back into the realm of the "It is done." You believe this, don't you? It is so stated in the law. But remember, anything that is stated in the law is not true so far as the human consciousness is concerned. It is all foolishness because it sets aside and overturns every belief of the human consciousness and, in so many words, destroys its kingdom.

The best weapon the human consciousness has against the Divine is derision. It laughs at the thought or the idea that a thing could happen before it is possible to happen, and it requires proof and demands that the shell of the egg be torn away in order to prove that the egg is changing form.

Remembering this, we see the power of the *secret* doctrine and why it is that you become as dumb as an ox led to slaughter, so far as discussing or telling anything pertaining to your ongoing or your understanding of the Word. Jesus once, in a moment of religious fervor, told things so high and mighty and so outside of the law that "they laughed him to scorn." So you see what is necessary in order that the "It is done" state of things may come to pass.

The "It is done" consciousness is the pure recognition of the Presence. It is entirely through with appearances and does not look for a sign. It does not need a sign, for it has the urge-feel that enables it to "go in and possess the land." It is all done the moment the acceptance is made.

Go in and possess the land, the consciousness of the New Idea. It is filled to the brim with a thrill that is pure bliss. No longer do you beg and beseech and wonder. Because of this recognition of the Presence and the going unto your Father-Consciousness, *you are now at the point* of going in and possessing the land that your fathers..., etc. It is wonderful, wonderful, wonderful!

You see now that the word of God, passing through the Father-Consciousness to you, "is quick, and powerful, and sharper than a two-edged sword," and it is this Word which shall decree a thing and it shall come to pass. You are told to "speak the word," but it says "the *Word*." It does not say the words of the man "whose breath is in his nostrils." It is a hook-up with the Word, the Logos, the *Only*, and this Word is sure of fulfillment. It cannot be spoken until you perceive the capacity of your Father within to contact the God-Almighty

Presence and thereby show forth the "It is done" state of things.

You are faced with a new deal, a lovely possibility of taking Jesus Christ at his word. His word is the Word. Do you realize that it is because of words that we have had so much trouble? The fact that we have so many words about God instead of *the Word* of God is what makes all the confusion and a thousand and one interpretations of the All-Presence. It accounts for all the towers of Babel that are constantly being erected.

Everybody who is still working on the "thought" way of attaining heaven is a builder of a tower of Babel because there is a diversity of opinions as to how it must be done; and after it gets piled high with word-bricks, the tower topples over onto the builders, and their many "tongues" cause such a jargon and fruitless confusion that the end is confounded misbelief.

"Gird up your loins" and arise into this New Day, backed by the power and force of the Fatherhood-Consciousness—which is yours the moment you recognize that you have within you this Father and that by reason of your contact with Him you make the complete Trinity—and the manifestation, which is "before you ask," comes into being. Yes, you shall "decree it, and it shall come to pass." Believest thou this? Believest thou that *I* am able to do this unto you? Answer Me!

The healing of the temple (body) which you have sought so long can be made possible only when you perceive the "It is done" state of consciousness. You can, no matter what the appearances are, accept your desire as "done" in consciousness. And the moment you come to that place, you are nearing the thin partition which separates the unmanifest from the manifest, and "in the twinkling of an eye" all is changed. Then you find yourself exclaiming, "Whereas before I was blind … now, now — *now* I can see," and you praise God from whom *all* blessings flow.

All these lovely things are happening to you as this book is being written. You do not yet know that it exists, because it has never come into your line of vision. But all this already exists, even though there is but half a page of the unfinished manuscript. Yes, it is complete and done and is being recorded for this very moment, when your eyes shall rest upon it and your heart exclaim, "My God and my Lord!"

The "It is done" state of consciousness takes from you all fear about results. "Even though you slay me, yet will I say you are God." Even if you slay me, I will recognize the Presence and the Power. And the "It is done" state of consciousness "stands and sees the salvation of the Lord." It is wonderful, wonderful, wonderful! Praise God from whom all blessings flow.

The "It is done" state of consciousness, brought about by recognition of the Trinity-unity, has no apprehension or anxiety. It does not look back, and it does not wonder how, where, or when this holy thing will take place. Everything is released, and the freedom of mind gives the new idea an easy and natural means of expression. The more natural and simple it is, the more it is possible to you. The birth of a babe in primitive tribes takes place without much bother or attention. The mother performs all the obstetrics herself and is back about her work in a few hours. No one thinks anything about it, other than that it is natural.

You remember what it takes to do all this? Do you believe? Can you put the seal of fire on your lips and *speak the Word* at the same time?

You see that the laws of God are past finding out by the human thought-taking consciousness because it has nothing upon which to base its premise. It is hopelessly sunk.

So what you are entering into is done, because you recognize this New Day and are beginning to glimpse the Father within, who is the point of contact with the universal Whole.

Chapter XVII

The Way of the Lord

Every valley shall be exalted, and every mountain shall be made low. The crooked places shall be made straight, and the rough places made smooth.

The highway, or the path of materialization, will be made easy and natural. No longer will the neophyte have to climb high "mental mountains" in order to contact the Lord. He will suddenly realize the Presence here, there, and everywhere and will learn the instant availability of the Lord.

It is wonderful when release has come to you from all the metaphysical tangle and jargon in which you have become enmeshed. All the ways and means and systems, all the mental, emotional trying to reach God in "high places" and all the strange practices used to know God will pass—and the way will be made smooth and natural and easy. Then you will know what it is to "go unto a high mountain" of consciousness.

It is not reached by a mental path but is a quick recognition of the Presence here, there, every-where—in the lowest dive, in the highest temple, in the midst of a brawl of mortal mind, in the midst of the sickly sense of peace and religious chatter, in anemic metaphysical talk. The Presence, with Its *way* of expression, is yours, and your recognition will bring Its flesh embodiment.

"My ways are not your ways." Suddenly, you are through with all the symbolic ways of Truth and come into the natural, normal way that the child can and does appropriate and use. To the child, Father Christmas is a real, live, flesh-and-blood being—an actuality; but to adult wisdom, he is just a symbol.

This same thing is true of the resurrected Jesus Christ, the "Word made flesh." It is no more a symbol; it is a reality—something which can be handled with the hands and something which eats and drinks and spreads about a joyous sense of all being well, something which fills the world with a spirit of light.

Benedictions fall like refreshing April showers, powerful enough to penetrate and soak the hard, parched soil. "These blessings I rain upon you," saith the Lord. This making the Word flesh, actually and naturally, is only possible to the one who believes in God. Again I repeat that almost everyone claims he does but immediately shows you that he believes more strongly in the devil. Evil seems to manifest itself so much more easily than good, and that is because *Christ in the flesh* has not been accepted.

If we are going to appropriate the gift of Jesus Christ, we cannot do it with the thinking mind, for we have already tried every possible way by that means. We will have to accomplish it from the place of recognition. The how, why, where, when must take care of itself. How it is to materialize and take unto itself a body is *none of our business.* Our business is to accept it, not only as possible but as already completed.

Now, all this *wisdom* of God, as revealed to us through Jesus Christ, is utter foolishness to the human mind; and likewise, all the wisdom of man is foolishness in the eyes of God. So what possible good will it do to try to appropriate with the limited human mind the unlimited gifts of Spirit? There is no possible way for this to happen.

Turn reason on the teaching of Jesus Christ, and it all melts into thin air and posits itself in a future state, after death. Turn reason on the Santa Claus fable, and he melts, too, into a myth. He turns into an actor and is not real, and ever after that, he becomes a mere symbol. But just once again *believe* in what Santa Claus stands for, and you will know your Father Noël to be flesh and blood. The "temple of God is with men," and the temple of God is the "stepper-down" of the gifts of Spirit.

That is why the habits formed in your consciousness through years of thought-taking metaphysics are all cast into the fire and consumed, for they are nothing but limitations.

The instant you become conscious of Me, there am *I* in the midst of you, and it does not require any mental rushing to some "high mountain." Before you can scale the peaks of the metaphysical high place, the Word has gone out and the results are there—that is, if you can *see*.

But the question arises, always, whether you can receive your good. So few can. Everybody thinks he is able to do so, but when it suddenly precipitates itself into his presence, he usually denies it. Perhaps he has not actually wanted it, and so the opportunity passes by. And if the person who turns away his good is not smart enough to cast the whole thing out of his consciousness, he will spend some time, maybe years, explaining how he was justified in not taking, when it came, the good for which he had asked.

Rest assured that what you ask for is coming by the way of God and not by the way of man. It will come through when the Power is ready to make it a reality to you. "My sheep hear my voice," and you have to come to the place of being alert and ready to move with, or accept, the good which you asked for, no matter how or when it comes into visibility.

"Watch, for you know not when the Son of man cometh." He cometh "as a thief in the night," in the silence and when least expected, for again I say, *the unexpected always happens.* It is wonderful that all the things you have asked for, and can really take, are yours without reservation, without limitation.

"Watching," is not looking for the manifestation. It is watching the "one hour" which is so important in the fulfillment of the big thing to be done. "Could you not watch with me one hour?" Stand fast in the consciousness of the "It is done," and the thing which the world calls miracle will take place.

"Refuse old wives' tales" is the advice of Timothy. Refuse the old, gossiping human belief that chatters about the Truth but knows nothing of the new revelation. What would they do with the Jesus if He were actually to come to them through the clouds? Crucify him again as a fake, no doubt. The old mortal thought that prates so much about the second coming of Jesus would put a short end to Him if He were to come again. He would have to be sponsored by some material organization to which He subscribed, or else He would be an "impostor."

Consider the words of Jesus; they are laws, fundamental and true. They can all be made manifest when you come to the place of recognition of the Presence. "Thou wilt keep him in perfect peace, whose mind is stayed on thee" is a statement of something that will actually take place, if you can understand through the new Light how to keep your mind stayed on *Him*. It is so wonderful and so simple—that in the midst of the confusion of material warfare is this peace possible and probable to him who will keep his mind stayed on the Father within. You have first to be convinced there is such a thing as the Father within. Are you satisfied that there is something in the universe bigger than your own pigmy intellect? And aren't you glad of it? Or are you?

The "old wives" are busy always, telling tales of failure and lack, sickness and death; and the idea of a "peace which passeth all understanding" is so abhorrent to them that they will do anything to make it impossible. The mortal mind is afraid of anything it cannot understand and immediately tries to destroy it. So all the lovely revelation of Jesus Christ was virtually wiped out by just this same group of old wives, which grouping, by the way, does not confine the "good work" to the feminine gender.

The leveling of all this pseudo-teaching, which enters into the mental realm and builds up all sorts of fantastic things to be done before God can be reached, is taking place in the individual. You will presently throw away all the old ideas that one must "work" or "do his work" in order to speak freely and naturally with God. This will become more apparent as you are able to recognize the presence of God in everything and everywhere and as indivisible. There are then not two of you — one matter and the other Spirit; there are not two voices, one material and the other spiritual; there are not two lives, one healthy and the other diseased.

All this separation is passing away as the Word becomes flesh, that is, as Spirit permeates matter and the two become one, as yeast and flour become one in a third substance called bread. Then are you *flesh*, and you are experiencing Oneness for the first time; then your voice is the God-voice, which speaks and it is done, because the transmutation has taken place and you are free.

All the "trying" to make this happen will only cause a greater separation between you and your Soul, or between matter and Spirit, for the mental, trying, knows at the outset that it is not true. And it is not true to the mental side of life.

Nothing is true to mortal man but that which he can "handle with his hands." He believes nothing that he cannot dissect and examine with his limited human knowledge. So in order to know Me aright, you must follow closely the simple instructions of Jesus Christ and be willing to cast away all human thought doctrines. Presently, you will actually find yourself truly believing in God. Much protest will arise over such a statement, but nevertheless, one day you will experience the "feel." You will actually *believe* in God, not because you were taught to do so or because you read the Bible, but because you have *become conscious* of this Presence.

All the fantastic teaching of the mental, which tries to make this difficult or slow of acquisition, is swept away by the Master, Jesus, when He deliberately and with abandon declares to mankind, "The works that I do, ye shall do also, and even greater than these shall ye do." Do you believe Jesus, or do you prefer to consult some high priest or priestess or to refer to a thick book or to some old papyrus found in the tomb of a near-heathen king?

What do you prefer to believe? Do you believe Jesus, or do you believe the John Smith of this century, who has a system of Truth that would try to put Jesus out of business unless He first prefaced His message with full credit to the same little John Smith. Is Jesus a truthsayer, or a liar?

What I want to find out is whether you believe in God or not. I keep asking you this because I want you to see this simple "oneness" of it all; how suddenly, everything that Jesus Christ said to us is possible and real and true and done—at the point of simplicity! When He spoke, He spoke with the God-voice. That was all there was with which to speak.

The double nature departs from your conscious-ness the moment the union of Spirit and matter has taken place. And this mystical union is just as natural as the coming of dawn. It has to be accepted as possible and natural—easy, natural, simple, and away from the emotional metaphysical labors that bring forth a child, or manifestation, with great acclaim, and with loud voice tell the world something is done that has never been done before and probably never will be done again, when in reality, the birth should be natural, normal, and in order. Everything in the kingdom of heaven is natural, normal, balanced, and in keeping with the law of harmony.

Make it all natural. Pull down these high mountains on which you have perched in emotional metaphysical unconsciousness and do away with these valleys of depression into which you have cast yourself every time you have perched as long as you could on the mountain. Make the highway of our Lord level; make it *one,* and speak with the one Voice and act with the one Power—and stop *trying to use* Me. I am you, and you are the medium, "flesh," through which *I* manifest.

Lo! When the mountains have been leveled and the valleys exalted and you travel the plains of peace and power, then shall you be able to come to the real Mountain of Transfiguration and Exaltation. Then shall you know heights which have no corresponding depths, for, in this new order, things do not go by pairs of opposites; there is no corresponding evil for the good you experience. But the human thought cannot take this in.

There shall be elevations
so wonderful and so high
that the imagination is lost
in fields of Light.

Chapter XVIII

Today

Today shalt thou be with me in paradise.

Said to the thief hanging on the cross; also said to you, hanging on the cross of your problem, the moment you can turn unto Me and ask of Me. Too good to be true; too wonderful, for, as is so tersely stated in the following lines:

> People have come to fear God. I think they fear Him more than they fear the devil. They have been told for so long that they are sinners, that all earthly pleasures are sent to lure them along the path to the burning pit, that they feel a greater fellowship with the Prince of Darkness than with the Lord of Hosts *(Life as Carola).*

There are thousands of mistaken souls today who think they are doing the Lord's work, when [actually] they are filling every passing soul with fear of life, stamping sin and evil all over the glorious universe.

It is wonderful to see how easily Jesus forgave the thief on the cross and how quickly He said to him, "Today shalt thou be with me in paradise." It is a beautiful contrast to the forgiveness of man. He forgives, or thinks he does, but he never forgets that he has saved or forgiven a sinner.

I once attended a large meeting in London where a pompous cleric bathed in the admiration of the audience over the sinners he had saved. He set himself up as a savior of men. He gave a long and glowing account of his work and then paraded in front of the audience a number of the saved ones. It was all so ghastly, this hypocrite who knew sin in everyone else except himself.

So through a hundred and one experiences, we begin to learn that to look to man is to lean upon a broken reed. "Turn ye even to me with all your heart," and "ye shall find rest for your soul." And so at the darkest and most fearful hour of any human experience, you can turn unto Me and hear the heartening words, "Today shalt thou be with me in paradise," and the sudden torture and hatefulness of the human picture disappears. It is all so impossible to put into words; and yet it can happen to you in the "twinkling of an eye" — not through thought, but by assumption of a new level of consciousness.

It is a fact that thousands of people feel a "fellowship with the Prince of Darkness" because after years of struggling, they have found it is easier to commit sickness than health, evil than good, and they have come to accept "when I would do good, evil I do" as a fact.

Then comes Jesus with the simplicity and truth of the Word — and most of all, Love, the Love that never faileth — and so the self-resurrection has begun. It has been a long trek back to the pristine beauty of "the image and likeness," but this return journey is fraught with such magnificent experiences as, "This day shalt thou be with me in paradise." Not tomorrow or next week, but *this day*—the day you can call upon Me and accept the light that is yours, regardless of what has gone before.

> Now, men are always supplicants to some outside power, for they have forgotten their own godliness. They pray to saints or try to invoke demons, but then do not look into their own hearts for Truth *(Life as Carola)*.

The way to paradise is through paradise. The state we are in now, no matter however troublesome it may have become through mismanagement, was heaven when we were in a lower degree. To begin to recognize this is to experience, in some degree at least, this instantaneous quality of the Word, "This day shalt thou be with me in paradise." When we begin to accept this new dimension of Jesus Christ, we will experience many things formerly thought impossible. This recognition, of going to heaven through heaven, explains in a measure the revelation of, "If you make your bed in hell (of human belief), I am there," and where *I* am, there is heaven.

It is always in the nature of revealing—never creating or changing, merely bringing greater *light*—and in this light we find things which we did not know existed, as the coming of day gradually breaks up great dark masses into many objects. Out of the darkness a rose garden may appear, but it was there all the while.

Gradually the differentiation between thought and consciousness takes place, and you begin to understand that the moment you enter into a given consciousness, you partake of everything that is indigenous to that level. By taking thought about it all, the best you can do is sometimes to reach up and take a single manifestation from the higher plane. But the next morning you are hungry again, and then you cannot find Me because you are still working with the uncertain thought-taking process.

Is it any wonder, then, that you are told to, "Be still, and know that I am God." "This day shalt thou be with me in paradise." "My grace is sufficient for thee."

> Do you hear? Do you begin to sense-feel the urge within you at the speaking of the *Word*? "This day shalt thou be with me in paradise."

Chapter XIX

Thou Art Not Far

Thou art not far from the kingdom of heaven.

You are so much nearer to it than you realize. The way of attainment is long, but the realization is "in the twinkling of an eye." You have come a long way through the reaches of human thinking and reasoning, and at last you are coming to the state of consciousness wherein you realize, "Thou art not far from the kingdom of heaven."

It is such a heartening thing, and somehow I feel like recording this for you, the reader. I feel impressed by the Spirit to say to you that this very lovely *Word* is being spoken *to you at this moment.* "Thou art not far from the kingdom of heaven." It is wonderful that I could set it down for you; and it is wonderful that you, this moment, sitting in your comfortable home or even in the gutter, can suddenly catch the full underlying significance of it and make it manifest. As swiftly as Light it comes into realization.

A sudden thrill comes to you as you realize the truth of the Word, "Thou art not far from the kingdom of heaven." Already you are bathed in the lovely light emanating from this Consciousness within you. It is well.

I Came

I am so glad to say
to you—yes, *you*:
"Thou art not far from
the kingdom of heaven."

Chapter XX

Karmic Law

O God! that one might read the book of fate,
And see the revolutions of the times
Make mountains level, and the continent,
Weary of solid firmness, melt itself into the sea ...
                                        —*Shakespeare*

When they asked Jesus, "Who did sin, this man or his parents, that he was born blind?" He answered, "Neither hath this man sinned, nor his parents, but that the works of God should be made manifest in him."

This wonderful revelation of the Christ-Power settles for always the hopeless straitjacket of karma from which the Orientals believe there is no escape. Jesus came to break the fate, or karmic patterns, by showing man the differentiation between shadow and substance. Finally, He lifted himself to a consciousness where He could not anymore be touched by belief.

His dismissal of the karmic belief was simple, as were all His other works. "The prince of this world cometh, and hath nothing in me." If there is nothing in you to respond to the false laws of the ancestors, the human fate, or karma, will have no place of expression. "Nothing happens but My love allows" takes care of all that when you have come to the point of recognition of the one Presence instead of two powers.

Nothing enters or finds a place of expression unless it is first accepted by you. It is true that you can accept a thing as real for another and manifest it yourself at a later date. You see now the necessity for your conversation to be, "Yea, yea" and, "Nay, nay."

"How did this happen to me?" is a common question. Somewhere along the line, you have accepted it as real for yourself, for another. This appears terrifying on the surface, but when you enter the revelation of Jesus Christ, many of the former things "shall not be remembered nor come into mind."

The idea of karma is not frightening once you have accepted Jesus Christ (the Word made flesh), the "flesh" in which you see God. "In my flesh shall I see God"—where God, Spirit, is stepped-down to a point of visibility through the agent of the temple-body.

Jesus functioned also in a karmic pattern but could at will move from his fate to his Divine Destiny. In other words, He neutralized the fate pattern with ease when He went unto his Father. He then arose to the elevation of the Father. The son, Jesus, was under the curse of the law just as you are until He discovered his true heritage and ascended to the Fatherhood degree.

There is no need for you to wonder at this power of transition, for it is resident in the mind of Christ Jesus, the identical mind which you are invited to *let be in you*. You, too, then have the capacity to transmute human fate and karmic laws, making them without power and virtually nil.

When you *repent*, you "turn" unto Me. In other words, you enter into a consciousness of the Christ. You transcend the laws of human belief—as surely as the Hebrew children transcended the laws governing flames and heat—and just as surely as you are told that from this elevation of consciousness the fire shall not burn, nor the water quench thee.

There are endless illustrations of the setting aside of human fate and thereby breaking the hypnosis of man. It is stated by Jesus Christ that, "Neither this man nor his father did sin." This sweeping statement puts to silence for all time the power of collective karma and fate. The hypnotic laws of the human mind will continue to be effective until the consciousness of the Christ is accepted.

"And if he drink any deadly thing, it shall not hurt him"—another proof that entering the consciousness of the Christ nullifies laws of the human mind. He does not in any way overcome karma, neither the laws of fire, water, poison. He is at a level where these things have no power. If he were to overcome them, he would have to endow them with power to hurt or kill him. He is not concerned about their disintegration or their appearances, even though he sees the same flames destroy the men who build the fires of supposed destruction, for *he is in the place where those laws are non-operative.*

If you have failed to accept the Immaculate Conception as a literal, actual, biological fact, as well as a symbolical law, you are still under the curse of karma because you have the conception of the woman, and your days are few and full of trouble. There is no escape from fate or karma through this heritage of the human belief; no escape but that which is worked out "by the sweat of your brow" and in the agony of the crucifixion and death on the human cross of belief.

Jesus submitted to this karmic picture to show you the great power of God to transcend all the beliefs of man, even death, knowing all the while that He could have neutralized the entire picture. But had He done this, we would still be without *proof.*

The emancipation of the soul from the prison house of fate and karma comes only through Self-Consciousness. This causes the mask of personality to give place to the Christ.

In the "overcoming" of disease and inharmony, man goes out to battle with something he declares is nothing—not unlike Don Quixote tilting at windmills, which he imagined an army of invaders. Likewise, when man establishes an "enemy," he must clothe it with a mask and give it or endow it with all the power it is going to have and to use against him.

As the *Self*-identification takes place in the individual, he experiences some of the things which have not been uttered by man, some of the things which Jesus could not tell in Jerusalem.

"There are many things I could not tell you because of your unbelief"—because of the incapacity to receive them, because of the belief in the limitations in the human mind. As we see Him ascending into the place of the Christ, we likewise see the flowing of the manifestation in terms that man can understand. Thus substance falls into loaves and fishes. It has always been there, but invisible to the human eyes that could not see. To make a thing appear which already is, is the work not of a mental magician but the capacity of him who speaks the *Word* without effort.

No wonder, then, Jesus said, "Leave all—follow me!" And gradually you are beginning to do just this. The consciousness is becoming so aware of the Presence, in which everything *is* and need not be "demonstrated" in the worn-out sense of the word, that the trifling demonstrations of the human thought are like so many gnats flying in the face of eternity.

The law is no respecter of persons. God does not bow to the will or desires of man. He is constantly functioning in all His glory, and it "falleth on the just and the unjust."

It is available to any man who will recognize it, and by his Self-identification with the Christ, he will experience it. All the valleys, depressions, and lack will be filled, and the hills of fear (the obstacles) be leveled.

Meditations

Enough and to Spare

There is "enough and to spare." Mean anything to you as a realization of the Word? Can you take it? Is it so? In any situation, any location, if you are conscious of it? Do you hear? "Enough and to spare." Notice there's *enough—and to spare.* Does it mean anything to you? How about a quiet half-hour on this revelation: "Enough and to spare."

Their Garments Waxed Not Old

Forty years in the desert, and their garments and shoes "waxed not old." Do you hear? Do you see?

In the popular slang of the streets, "What goes on?" Here we have something *not* to think about, for it is a lie and never did or could happen in thought. Thought in its highest form is based on the findings of science and its laws, one of which is that friction will wear anything out, disintegrate it, do away with it. So you cannot think about forty years' use of a garment or a pair of shoes and still think that they wax not old. That could only happen in a fairy tale; and so ... and so ... and so ... and in reality it can only happen in a story of God written for a child-consciousness that can and does transcend the laws of science and scientific thinking. It just cannot happen in thought. But it does happen in consciousness, and that is the place of conception.

Enter in then and close the door, and "the Father who seeth in secret shall reward thee (not you and somebody else, but you) openly"—but don't you dare tell it or cut it to pieces with the curious human thought.

Can you spare Me (or watch with Me) one hour in the contemplation of: their garments and their shoes "waxed not old for forty years"?

187

Behold

To sense the word *behold* is to cause a sudden releasement of invisible Light in which you will see the things which have not yet been seen or heard of, nor have entered into the heart. "Behold, I (*I am* God) make all things new." You cannot think of it, for there is too much matter to dispose of, too much congested thought to do away with; so if you are to get in on this wonderful revelation, you will have to do it beyond the place of human thinking. You will literally have to *behold*—be so conscious of the Presence that everything is lost and completely forgotten. This you can and will do when you are ready. Do you hear?

Like running straight into the dawn—half an hour of this contemplation will make you luminous, a temple of Light.

.

Created

You were *created*. All you have to do is *remember* this to do something about the evil conditions in the body "born of woman ... full of trouble" and sin and its pictures. You were *created* perfect and changeless; so glance or look again at this "picture shown to you on the mount," and you will find the desert blossoming as a rose; the waste places shall be made glad.

Can you watch with Me a few moments on this, in contemplation? Be sure you don't think about it — contemplate Me in breathless adoration.

Instant Protection

The way of instant escape from evil lies in the Jesus Christ Consciousness. Jesus showed this protection a hundred times in His ministry and finally virtually defied His persecutors with the question:

> Think ye not that I could call upon my Father, and he would send me twelve legions of angels?

A legion was six thousand infantry besides the cavalry. Just imagine the fiasco that would have taken place if, instead of mentioning the idea, He had actually called upon his Father. I cannot imagine any legion of man-made power wanting to attack a single Angel of Power, let alone *a legion.*

And remember, "The things I do, *ye* shall do also, and even greater." You have this power too— that is, if you will enter into your God-given heritage, above the thought-taking plane, and "speak as one having authority." Do you begin to understand a little?

When these invisible twelve legions of angels are called into manifestation, they form such an invisible power that anything attempting further human evil is consumed, just as the men who built the fire for the Hebrew children were consumed, while it had no effect on the Hebrew children. This speaking of *the invisible twelve legions of angels* into expression is the calling on the Father-Consciousness, which is the point through which all God-power is released on earth.

When you are *enfolded* in this wall of protection, you are safe from whatever evil the human mind has concocted against you. "No weapon (not any) that is formed against you shall prosper." Do you hear? Do you believe? "Every tongue that is incensed against thee shall be put to shame."

The evil human mind that would persist in offering evil after you had called forth the twelve legions of angels would find himself dashed hopelessly against a wall of destruction. His open sword of attack would be telescoped like a corkscrew if he tried to use it, and his mental weapons would suddenly turn and run him through. He would be happy even to escape to his place of complete idiocy of the human mind.

"They will come at you in one way"—with all their power of human law and the wickedness of the mortal mind—"and they shall flee in ten."

This is not a legend. It is a law of Consciousness, and you can set it in action *the moment* you make your contact with the Father and *allow* your body to be the temple of the living God.

"Fear not, for I am with you" then takes on a new meaning. It carries with it a power of which no human mind has ever dreamed, against which nothing shall stand. Do you hear?

All the old karmic debt of evil — all the vicious-ness and jealousy of the human mind that is turned against you — shall be withered away, and if the man thinks he can yet stand against It, give him his chance. Like a stupid night bird that hurls its weight and speed against a lighthouse, he is literally dashed to pieces and drops into the Sea of Oblivion.

So be it with every evil thing or person who stands in the way of the Light. You have your protection with you, for, "I am with you always." The Heavenly Host stands guard as the twelve legions accomplish the total destruction of the vicious human mind that attempts evil *for its last time.*

"Fear thou not, for I am with you."

To the Poor

To the poor the gospel is preached.

In the orthodox sense of the word, it seems rather a slim chance of anything happening. Why not give the poor riches, or at least *something,* so they can get on? Because the consciousness of poverty could never be helped by giving it things. It is a barrel with a hole in it that is bigger than any stream of substance which could be poured into it.

Without the *consciousness* of substance, nothing can be had or accumulated. As long as the "poor" consciousness remains, there is nothing on the *outside* that can be done that will in anyway benefit the poor but temporarily.

The meaning of "the gospel is preached" is that the revelation of the true state of affairs is explained. By preaching the gospel—the good-spell—finally the poor man begins to see that instead of being dependent upon another, he has infinite resources within himself. He begins to discover that he too is created equal from the standpoint of Spirit, and the moment he moves into this state, he begins to assume and partake of his equality in all lines.

The first thing that happens when this recognition comes to the poor is an automatic stopping up of the hole in the barrel. Almost without fail, the mental attitude of begging and beseeching and dramatizing poverty will fall away. Instead of trying to make other people believe in his poverty and wretchedness, the dignity and pride of man's heritage comes into play, and he goes within and "shuts the door" (the hole) and prays to the Father, the Permanent Identity; and the Father, seeing in secret, rewards openly.

Thus, when the son returns from the contact with the Father to his place of expression, he begins to find that things are changing and that he is moving or ascending to a place of recognition of the Presence, in the fullness of which are all things. He likewise understands how it is that "the gospel is preached" to the poor.

Giving must not be withheld, even to "the poor," when the occasion demands; but the continual feeding of the poor in consciousness accomplishes nothing; for every time it is full, it goes to sleep in a momentary contentment and awakens as hungry as ever with nothing to eat and must again forage and dramatize its poverty and lack—an endless chain of evil.

With this recognition of truth comes the joy of self-sufficiency—the clean, free state of things that makes for happy living and that eventually places the one on the path of supplying his brother's need. It is wonderful, for the moment you realize this state of things, you also have automatically functioned e law of substance. If you are to supply your brother's need, you must automatically have something with which to supply it.

It seems involved at first, this escaping from the prison cell of poverty, but it is easier than it appears—a sudden arising, a sudden reliance on the Power, a sudden forgiving of one's self, and a taking away the condemnation that has been placed there.

Those who followed Jesus into the desert—many of them were poor (in consciousness), and in spite of the "preaching" and the demonstration of substance, they remained that way. They came again for food and finally earned the stern rebuke, "You seek me for the loaves and fishes, and not because of the miracle." In other words, you were "preached to"—the *gospel* was given you, that which would have freed you into abundance—but you saw only the manifestation of that preaching and are empty constantly.

"Awake thou that sleepest, and Christ will give thee light." That is a gift which must be accepted, too. It is given unto you the moment you are ready to accept it. But unless you can recognize that it is a gift, there is little use trying to accept something that does not exist. You see then what is required when we pray (in the consciousness), "believing that we have already received."

All this symbology will be made perfectly plain to you when you are ready to break with the old ideas and take on the new. "Be absent from the body," the body of poverty thoughts, long enough to appropriate your own heritage. Arise from the debris of human bondage and thoughts and go unto the Father-Consciousness. "Before you ask, I will answer" cannot be made true by affirmations or treatments. *It is already true,* and until you discover this, you will keep trying to make it true and will fail. When you can begin with the "belief" that it is already true, half of the battle is over—more than half, for it is only then necessary to *let* this wonderful gift find a way and means into expression through your body-temple.

How will it come? No man knows. The more impossible it is, the easier it is with God. "All things are possible to God," and God is the great universal Spirit over all, in all, and is the only reality in the universe, the only thing which changes not and which does not pass away.

So one day, as the gospel is being preached to the poor, something will happen. He will open his eyes a degree farther than he has yet known and *see* how it is that the "things prepared" cannot be created anymore, but must be released. Endless arguing, demonstrating, trying to trick either yourself or God result in a fatigue and futility that eventually turns entirely away from God. "It didn't work; I tried so hard to make a go of it; I studied, etc., etc."

It didn't work because it is not supposed to "work," and most of all, no man can "work" God. He is not a machine that is played by dropping a nickel in the slot. A man-made prayer or a recommended affirmation will not cause the wheels of the universe to turn around and give forth a hatful of nickels. As long as you have this idea, you take with it also the high percentage of loss of the slot machine. The chances of a jackpot are so remote it is hardly worth the effort.

Awake and arise from this sluggish thing called poverty and enter into the consciousness of God. "When you are ready, *I* will do the works through you." Do you hear? When *you* are *ready*—when you are willing and will let this wonderful thing happen to you. Suddenly the gospel is preached and you hear it, and you then know the wonderful wisdom in the law, "to the poor the gospel is preached." That is the only way of freedom from the poor-consciousness.

Blessed Are the Meek

The hypnosis of this statement when taken from the human standpoint is already too well known to make further comment. Thousands of people, many sincere but many insincere, have thought by being "meek" they would inherit the earth. Later on—a good deal later—they find they have inherited nothing but the backwash of life and that their diet is composed of the crumbs under the table.

The self-effacing martyrdom of many people who believe they are being meek is pathetic, and yet many of them believe sincerely that it is the command of God to make themselves the doormats of the universe.

Nothing could be further from it. When Jesus "turned the other cheek," it was not from the "hang dog" state of mind, but from the supreme consciousness of the Power that lay in it. He knew that if the other cheek were slapped, it would be the everlasting end of the one who did the slapping. We apparently can trifle with the laws of God to a certain degree; but one day the meek thing you have been kicking around will turn the other cheek, and then you are on the spot.

The moment the Jesus Christ Consciousness comes into being, then it is just as well that nothing in human form or human thought tries to slap the other cheek. Suddenly the meek thing has become the tower of strength and fire.

"My sheep hear my voice." It doesn't matter about anything else—but because they hear My voice, they obey, and in this obedience are they given the power of meekness. The high and mighty may appear dangerously near to destroying the meek, but all of a sudden the other cheek is turned, and then the game is finished. Subtle and unseen powers, with which he is wholly unable to cope, begin his undoing by a way he knows not of. He discovers that he is in the garden where he does not belong and that he is "naked." So is it with all the evil of the universe that is desperately trying to make a last stand.

The meek are the people who remain silent and let the "big voice" that knows it all tell everything. The wise one remains meek while the power and energy of the adversary is wasted in a thousand and one ways. He knows to "know nothing" is to know everything, but if he tells it to everybody, then it becomes nothing. A secret is a powerful thing, but it is no secret when it is told and has no further power. So the meek remain meek and unassuming until they are to speak of the glory of God, and that will be after they have inherited the earth.

What earth? Their earth! We all have an earth of our own—it is our conception of what "the earth" means to us. Like a radio program—we can all have it and yet all be left; and we have choice and

199

selectivity, mixed or unmixed with static and interference, brought forth on a good machine or an inferior one.

Do you begin to see that in the consciousness we have all, and yet all is left—and this is all "foolishness" in the eyes of man—and so it is. We are not "taking thought" on anything like this. It has to be revealed in consciousness, and then the Light-thought will flow from that Consciousness and cause us to perceive many things.

Yes, the meek shall inherit the earth, and this inheritance is worth having. So be meek. "Salute no man" on the highway of Life. Don't discuss the power of God for the sake of an argument, or else you will come out the loser.

Flee from the man "whose breath is in his nostrils," because he wants to compare notes, and he "knows everything" anyway—which is *nothing*. There is a sure check on this. "By their works shall ye know them." If they haven't any works, they haven't anything to say to you—and this needs the high consciousness of God to interpret, since at the very same time, they may have no things—yet you will see and understand "what the Spirit says unto the churches."

"Keep silent before me." Don't tell Me what to do, and don't tell Me what you need. *I* know all your needs before you ask. You only have to permit this Light to come through into manifestation, Light that, through the consciousness of *meekness*, will show you the "earth" you are to inherit.

Yes, "the meek shall inherit the earth."

Shedding of the Blood

Except by the "shedding of the blood," the inheritance could not come. The will could not be probated unless the price had been paid. Jesus came and, literally as well as symbolically, paid the price; but the heirs didn't see it was the time to probate the will of God and take their inheritance. "Awake! Arise and shine, for thy light is come, and the glory of God is risen upon thee."

You are an heir and a joint-heir, and the blood has been literally and symbolically shed. "Go in and possess the land" now, for you understand why you are able to do this, just as you also must understand why "the cattle on a thousand hills are mine."

By the shedding of the blood (the blessed inspiration of the Jesus Christ Consciousness) do you realize the actual right you have to the kingdom of heaven. You begin to sense-feel that you are an heir—yes, an heir with Christ, with the same Consciousness which was also in Jesus. You are a joint-heir with everyone who recognizes this wonderful Consciousness within him.

The consummation took place, and the blessed blood was shed, and the inspiration was released. The flowing wine was given to all who would partake.

"Call no man your father upon the earth: for one is your Father, which is in heaven." And again you see what it means to recognize this divine birth, this immaculate conception. It verifies the probating of the will of God. You suddenly begin to realize that you are the heir, for you have come from under the cloud of being the child of the bond-wife (human Adamic creation) and are the legitimate heir to the riches of the kingdom. Enter in!

The urge you have felt for so long to possess riches was then quite true and real, though passed through the glass darkly of human thought. It was so distorted and ugly as to produce every kind of dishonesty.

You are free born.

In the Beginning

The Greeks went back to chaos. The Buddhists went back to "the great nothingness," "the great emptiness." The Christian goes back to "the void."

"The earth was without form and void." From this point of the unformed were all things made that were made to appear. When the great Revelator, Jesus Christ, said, "Before Abraham was, I am," He went back to a point beyond any form or shape of human thinking. He went back to *the Father*. The Father was not a man, but the great Void out of which all things came into being. It is the glory *I* had with thee before the world of John Smith appeared.

As the child takes its bucket to the sea and brings back the formless sea in the shape of the bucket, so Jesus inferred that, "whatsoever" He asked the Father — whatsoever *shape of consciousness* He took to the Father, or Sea, would be filled, or stepped-down to a point of visibility. As the sea which the child brings back in the shape of a bucket will only remain in that shape as long as the bucket holds it, so did Jesus know that when the thing was released in consciousness, it would return to the *One* again, to be reshaped anew by the *asking* consciousness.

There could be no begging the sea to get into the shape of the bucket, and hence, there could be no beseeching and affirming that the Father take the shape of health or happiness or money. The consciousness would have to present that shape to the Father and that too without the slightest question as to whether it were possible or not.

Any questioning as to whether it could or could not happen would only mar or destroy the shape of consciousness. Repetition would destroy the essential faith. Any beseeching and begging and treating would show the hypocrisy of man endeavoring to impress God with his spirituality — as if God, who created you, is not well aware that you are pure Spirit and as if He did not know the "need" before you asked.

Small wonder, then, that the instructions were after this fashion: "When ye pray, believe that ye receive." This is not done at the insistence of willpower. Any willpower is an indication that you do not believe but hope by the force of human thought to make God do something He has not already done.

When you enter into prayer after this fashion, it will be from *recognition* and not from the standpoint of hypocrisy that imagines it can do things with God. Psychology is not prayer.

Once a thing has taken shape and form, it is finished. Nothing can be added or taken from it, as it were. It cannot be reshaped any more than a vase, after it has come from the kiln, can be refashioned. Healing does not take place on the body; the new *shape of consciousness* automatically brings with it the new *shape of manifestation.*

No wonder, then, that Jesus left all form behind and entered into the place of *unformed Spirit.* What He told the Father in secret was called from the housetop. He could do nothing with the "dead" child. "I go to awaken him." Jesus was not an overcomer; and yet today there are thousands trying to overcome sin, disease, and death. Jesus left the pictures behind when He went to the Father with His *shape of consciousness.* No wonder, then, Lazarus came forth and was unbound of the graveclothes.

Beyond the picture of you, there is that from which you say you sprang—your father; and back of him, his father; and back of him, his father. But after you have played with this childish assignment long enough, you realize that back of the first so-called father is *the Father.* When we want to get into the flow of it, we will see what Jesus meant when He said, "Call no (not any) man your Father." Now this takes on a definite meaning, for the various shapes and forms that you have called *father* are not *the* Father, but manifestations of the Father.

If you partake of the qualities of your personal father, you will have all his foibles and beliefs to handle. If the sea were to become the same quality as the water in the bucket that has been left to stand for months or years in the same shape, it would surely be dead.

We find, then, that going to *the Father* is going to the infinite Source of all substance, and whatsoever Jesus asked was called from the housetops. "Call upon me, and I will answer you," takes on a different meaning. Dip your bucket into the sea and carry away the exact measure you have accepted as a reality—not what you hoped for, not what you tried to demonstrate, but what you *accepted as a reality!*

Back of every manifest thing is that *Something*, the Power, which is not subject to the laws of the manifest but upon which the manifest thing is dependent.

Why, then, will man persist in taking thought and repeating words? A whole symphony is in a single note. A complete revelation could be in a single word, *if* it were heard. When you pray, it is not with words or argument but with *pure recognition*; and could you but wait a split second, you, too, could say with Jesus, "Thank you, Father," for the finished thing, and the signs would automatically follow.

The Hour of Silence

Remember the day on which, without fear in your heart, you met your first silence. The dread hour had sounded; silence went before your soul. You saw it rising from the unspeakable abysses of life, from the depths of the inner sea of horror or beauty, and you did not fly ... .

Bethink you of that moment ... and tell me whether silence, then, was not good and necessary, whether the caresses of the enemy you had so persistently shunned were not truly divine.

—Maurice Maeterlinck

The last, and I might say the first, enemy you will have to settle accounts with is yourself. The most difficult period of life is the *aloneness*—when you come face to face with this *self* who has become swollen through a thousand incarnations and who has had the whip hand for eons.

That is why so few people can stand to be alone. They do not want to meet this monster. It is only when you can stay with him for a while that you finally discover the heel which is vulnerable and can destroy him with his bag of tricks—with his ancestor teaching and beliefs garnered from appearance. It is only when you face the "liar, and the father of it" with some of his lies that he takes cover. "Who did hinder you, that you should not obey the truth?" You have the answer to this now.

And who is it that told you you were naked and therefore ashamed? Why ashamed?

It is wonderful when this old demon is re-valued and found to be a pack of lies and discovered to be utterly powerless once you have taken your thought away from him. He deflates like a balloon punctured by a pin. And then the Alone place is the place of *revelation*—the place where the extended senses take over, and you begin to see and hear and understand some of the new dimensions, and more especially, you begin to understand the "reason for the hope that is within thee."

There is a purpose for the God-created You. It is not just following the successful path of your forebears, going through a series of meaningless pictures, fooling yourself with the idea you are getting somewhere, only to find you have come out at the same place you went in.

> Myself when young did eagerly frequent,
> Doctor and Saint and heard great argument
> About it and *about*; but evermore
> Came out the same door wherein I went.
> —Omar Khayyam

There is a purpose in Life which is sadly missing in the life of the Adam dreamer. "Ye must decrease" is spoken to this thought-production so that the *I* (the eternal Being) will again increase into His full stature and find out the purpose of being. It is glorious and golden when we begin to sense the Life beyond the life and see that It is continuous and eternal and has an infinite field of action. Discovering the true Self, we find we are sent for a purpose; we are sent a Light, and this releasing of Light is so great it reveals the purpose of being.

Papers are full of stories of successful men, how they have slaved, worked night and day, gone through all sorts of hells, and finally amassed a fortune and died. No wonder the Preacher said, "Vanity of vanities, all is vanity." Yes, all is vanity and illusion; and the deluge of words, optimistic as they may seem, has no power to change this futility and frustration. "Could ye not watch with me one hour?" The willingness to fold the tent and steal away into the desert and be alone, away from teacher, preacher, book, and lecture, is replete with results.

Suddenly, after you have faced this chimera that seems so terrible on the outside, you begin to see right through and see the mass of thoughts you have stored up as real, which are merely accepted beliefs inflated and made real by acceptance and then brought into activity by race-consciousness. If you believe in evil and the race-consciousness is particularly rampant on that subject at the moment, you are carried right along into the thick of the battle.

Maybe you will emerge somewhat the worse for it all, but the chances are you may not. Until you accept a thing, it cannot come into being; yet the moment you do, you find agreement which results in establishing it on the earth. "It shall not come nigh thee" is said of the one who has not accepted the belief and is therefore above the line of the activity of race-consciousness.

Everything that the human thought has tried to do from its level of initiation and hypnosis can and will be carried through into manifestation by the *Self*—the Christ of God which you have discovered by being alone.

The alchemy of the medieval philosopher and wise man gives way to the revelation of Spirit, which actually can and does have the power of changing disease into health, limitations into abundance, and sorrow into joy—not as a magician does it, but as the Son of the most High reveals the stream of spiritual Light descending into the crooked shapes of human thought and disintegrating them.

It is wonderful. It is secret. And it is done not for show and not for a price, but for the automatic results that follow pure recognition of the Presence. A child can or could do it, and so can you—if you can.

The magic of doing "tricks," called miracles by the human thought, is intriguing, but how can a power that can walk through fire, water, solid walls, etc., function in a mind that is filled with the egotism of the little Adam-self? The inside of the platter must be made clean before it is a fit receptacle to receive anything. And this does not bespeak the terrible struggle and overcoming so often pictured with it; it does bespeak of a mind that has arrived at a place where it really believes in something higher, greater, and more powerful than all the combinations of human thought, no matter how time-honored. It is wonderful and glorious. When you think about it, you want to do something, want to shout for joy or throw your hat in the air.

And so you meet your first *silence*, which is not a mumbling of sanctimonious words of a man, but an actual surcease from words, ideas, preconceived notions, and desires; a steady gazing into the Light until you are swallowed by It.

You are in the Silence *now,*
and that which is told you
shall be called from the housetops.
It is wonderful!

About the Author

Walter Lanyon was highly respected as a spiritual teacher of Truth. He traveled and lectured to capacity crowds all over the world, basing his lectures, as he said, "solely on the revelation of Jesus Christ."

At one point, he underwent a profound spiritual awakening, in which he felt "plain dumb with the wonder of the revelation." This enlightening experience "was enough to change everything in my life and open the doors of the heaven that Jesus spoke of as here and now. I know what it was. I lost my personality; it fell off of me like an old rag. It just wasn't the same anymore."

His prolific writings continue to be sought out for their timeless message, put forth in a simple, direct manner, and they have much to offer serious spiritual seekers.

Walter Clemow Lanyon was born in the U.S. on October 27, 1887, and he passed away in California on July 4, 1967.